The
Medical Value
of
Psychoanalysis

Classics in Psychoanalysis

Edited by
The Chicago Institute For Psychoanalysis
George H. Pollock, M.D., Ph.D.,
President

Monograph 2

The
Medical Value
of
Psychoanalysis

By Franz Alexander, M.D.

International Universities Press, Inc.
New York   •   New York

Library of Congress Cataloging in Publication Data

Alexander, Franz Gabriel, 1891-1964.
    The medical value of psychoanalysis.

    (Classics in psychoanalysis; monograph 2)
    Reprint. Originally published: New York: W.W. Norton,
c1936.
    Includes index.
    1. Psychoanalysis. 2. Psychotherapy. 3. Medicine,
Psychosomatic. 4. Personality. I. Title. II. Series:
Classics in psychoanalysis; monograph no. 2.
    [DNLM: 1. Psychoanalysis. W1 CL122D no. 2 /
WM 460 A375m 1936a]
RC506.A44 1984   616.89'14   84-22475
ISBN 0-8236-3285-7
ISSN 0735-0341

Manufactured in the United States of America

TO
SIGMUND FREUD

CONTENTS

The
Medical Value
of
Psychoanalysis

Foreword

The Chicago Institute for Psychoanalysis is delighted to have this classic reissued as part of its Classics in Psychoanalysis series. It is of historic significance but also of current importance when psychoanalysis and psychiatry are re-examining their roots in and connections with the field of medicine. We hope the reader will benefit from the insights of over fifty years ago.

In 1931, the first edition of *The Medical Value of Psychoanalysis* by Franz Alexander, the founder of the Institute for Psychoanalysis of Chicago, appeared. In the second edition, published five years later, Alexander gives credit to his collaborating colleagues: Drs. Catherine Bacon, Thomas French, Margaret Gerard, Edwin Eisler, Harry B. Levey (Lee), Maurice Levine, Helen McLean, Karl Menninger, William Menninger, George Mohr, Leon Saul, Lucia Tower, and George Wilson. I mention these names of some of our founding pioneers because they represent the past and to a lesser extent the present.

3

Even though the volume is over half a century old, it is fresh with ideas that have significance today. And although the volume deals with the relationship of psychoanalysis and medicine, the ideas expressed so clearly can be applied to the relationship of psychoanalysis to psychiatry. Alexander's description of the nature of psychological understanding is still valid today. The "chief instrument is a kind of identification with the other person, that is, a putting of one's self in the other person's mental situation. If you observe the movements of another, the expression of his face, the tone of his voice, and if you listen also to what he says, you get an idea of what is going on in his mind. This understanding is derived from the fact that the object of observation is a being similar to the observer—both are human personalities. This similarity between observer and observed is quite essential" (pp. 32-33). Alexander goes on to note that "In psychological observation the external behavior of the observed object is supplemented by direct or introspective knowledge of one's own person. The importance of this coexistence of objective and introspective observation in psychology cannot be stressed enough" (p. 33). Alexander makes the point that this mode of observation is the basis of psychoanalysis, and later he extended his belief to dynamic psychiatry.

Earlier in the book, Alexander observed that "If psychoanalysis had remained . . . a modest technical device in psychotherapy, the question of its belonging to medicine would never have been raised" (p. 11); but since "it has developed a dynamic theory of personality, it came to have a bearing on all sciences which deal with the products of the mind" (p. 11) and so psychoanalysis cannot be claimed by medicine (and I would add psychiatry) alone. But the contribution of psychoanalysis to the idea that man is a bio-psycho-social entity is a major contribution and as Alexander pointed out it opened for us the domain for future investigation of the detailed interrelationship of physiological (I would add biochemical and pharmacological), socio-cultural-economic, historical, and psychological processes. We are already witnessing the revolution introduced by our greater understanding of chemical neuro-transmitters and endocrine substances, thus bearing out Freud's earlier suggestion of a bio-psychological organism.

What are the other contributions of psychoanalysis to psychiatry that Alexander delineated over fifty years ago? Are they still valid today?

1. The theory of catharsis and its relationship to psychotherapy. Valid today.

2. The discovery of the method of free association and how this helped us understand the meaning of symptoms. Here again the observer hears the associations and makes order out of them. Valid today.

3. The theory of repression and of unconscious mental processes. Valid today.

4. The discovery of infantile sexuality. Valid today.

5. The theory of instincts. Interestingly, here Alexander singles out narcissism for special emphasis. In an interesting footnote (p. 71), he quotes from Shaw's *Heartbreak House*. "Captain Shotover says: 'A man's interest in the world is only the overflow from his interest in himself. When you are a child your vessel is not yet full; so you care for nothing but your own affairs. When you grow up, your vessel overflows; and you are a politician, a philosopher, or an explorer and adventurer. In old age the vessel dries up: there is no overflow: you are a child again' " (p. 71). Partially valid today.

6. The oedipus complex. Valid today.

7. The development of ego psychology, including the structural point of view and the tripartite

model of the psyche. Valid today.

8. The investigation of dreams. Valid today.

9. Intrapsychic conflict. Valid today.

10. The theory of symptom-formation. Valid to-day.

11. Transference. This kind of relationship Alexander notes develops spontaneously in any form of psychotherapy (and we know this is true of all human relationships). Valid today.

12. The psychoanalytic therapeutic model. Here again Alexander keenly observes that "Psycho-analysis does not claim to be able to cure all forms of mental disturbances or all kinds of pathological personalities. It only maintains that all future meth-ods of psychotherapy must be based on an under-standing of the fundamental psychodynamic processes. . . . An insight into fundamental psy-chodynamic structure is the principal contribution of psychoanalysis to psychiatry" (p. 105). Valid to-day.

In the section on the psychoanalytic treatment of the psychoses, Alexander, using an ego psycholog-ical model, weaves in the contributions of Melanie Klein, Anna Freud, Brill, Zilboorg, Sullivan, Nun-berg, and of course Freud. Alexander points out that psychoanalytic knowledge helps us understand the psychoses, but that traditional psychoanalytic therapy is inappropriate in treating schizophrenics. Instead he believes a new and modified technique of psychotherapy will be used in the "future" in the care of such patients. Again an interesting footnote: "the importance of psychogenic factors is not the same in all cases of manic-depressive disturbances" (p. 111). Hence not all patients with this diagnosis can be treated with psychoanalytic treatment. We have now elaborated on this idea. Lithium treats the manic-depressive disturbance, and psychoanalytic psychotherapy can be used in the therapy of the other disturbances that may be present at the same time as the manic-depressive illness. In other words, an individual can have two or more psychic disorders at the same time, each of which requires a different treatment.

Alexander's chapter on "Psychic Influences on Body Functions" lays the groundwork theoretically and clinically for his later pioneering work in psychosomatic medicine. We find current work on stress and coping, behavioral and holistic medicine as direct descendants of the very important insights Alexander expressed years ago. I found the references to the work of E. Simmel and Felix Deutsch and Flanders Dunbar, as well as the clinical reports of the Chicago team, interesting and still excitingly relevant. It is fascinating to compare the formulations of 1936 with what we observe in our ongoing work in psychosomatic correlations.

The final chapter deals with "Psychoanalysis in Medical Education." Alexander reviews how psychoanalytic education developed in modern psychoanalytic institute organizations from the early pioneers who founded the first psychoanalytic institute in Berlin in 1920. This chapter has references to psychiatric education as well as the outline of the Berlin curriculum and how it was introduced into the Chicago Institute and, I might add, some elements of this curriculum are still used.

Much of what Alexander had to say forty-eight and fifty-three years ago has relevance for us today—not all of the past is gone and has to be dismissed out of hand. We do indeed stand on some shoulders of some giants to see and provide shoulders for our future generations.

GEORGE H. POLLOCK, M.D., PH.D.
President, Chicago Institute for Psychoanalysis

January, 1984

Preface to the First Edition

THE place of psychoanalysis among the sciences is a question which, in the course of the last decade, became even more problematic than it was in those early days when Freud and a small group of his followers, with the help of a new psychological technique, tried to cure certain cases of so-called "nervous" disturbances. If psychoanalysis had remained such a modest technical device in psychotherapy, the question of its belonging to medicine would never have been raised. Since, however, it has developed a dynamic theory of personality, it came to have a bearing on all sciences which deal with the products of the mind. At present psychoanalytical psychology cannot be claimed by medicine alone. But its relation to medicine itself has changed since the analytic therapy has been based more and more on the knowledge of pathological mental processes and on certain general dynamic and structural assumptions concerning the make-up and functioning of the personality.

With the development of analytic theory, it has become increasingly clear that psychoanalysis is an essential contribution to medicine, and forces us to revise certain fundamental concepts in medicine and biology. I do not think, however, that medicine need resent such a revaluation of its methods and fundamental assumptions, since the revaluation of basic scientific concepts is a typical feature of our present age. The critical movement began with physics, whereas medicine was for a long time spared this kind of revolution. The principle that the phenomena of life can be reduced to physico-chemical processes—a view which was unquestionably responsible for the speedy progress in biology and medicine during the last fifty years—dominated and directed medical thinking from its beginnings as a natural science. I do not think that this principle is endangered by the new psychological approach to biological phenomena, although this new approach offers fundamentally new aspects. In the first place, it makes a more general application of the dynamic point of view possible than the one-sided somatic analysis of the processes of life. Not the validity but the exclusiveness of the somatic analysis of biological phenomena seems to be shattered.

This book is mainly an attempt to clarify the problematic relation of psychoanalysis to medicine, though in the chapter on "Psychogenic Factors" I try to go further and discuss the question of the significance of psychoanalytical principles for biology in general.[1] It is also an attempt to dissipate the prejudice against psychoanalysis in biological and medical circles, among those who feel that the introduction of psychological views into medicine threatens to reduce the exact nature of this youngest of the natural sciences. The aims of the book, therefore, make it important to give a clear and systematic presentation of the methodological and theoretical concepts which are generally accepted and considered as fundamental in the present system of psychoanalysis.

I must confess that I have felt a systematic presentation, such as I tried to give in the first two chapters, to be most difficult. The gradually increasing insight into the make-up and functions of the mind, which has been gained in the last ten years, has led to a consistent theory of human personality which, however, has not yet been formulated in an organized and systematic fashion. The incompleteness and some of the defects of my presentation may be excused by the novelty of my undertaking. I feel, however, that in the first chapter I have succeeded in formulating the fundamental characteristics of the psychoanalytical method in a way that may perhaps satisfy even the requirements of an epistemological treatise. In the second chapter, in which I have described the present

[1] In this new edition this chapter is replaced by two new chapters: V "Psychic Influences on Body Functions," and VI "Recognition of Psychic Factors in Modern Medicine."

status of psychoanalytic theory, I have tried to restrict myself to what seemed to me essential as well as empirically best founded. This may explain the impression of incompleteness which especially the trained psychoanalyst may receive in reading this part of the book. In this chapter my aim has been to express the intimate relation of the therapeutic concepts to the more general theory and to show that the knowledge of psychological processes which is gained during treatment is the solid basis both of analytic theory and therapy. Whatever changes theory and therapeutic technique may undergo in the future, the description of the psychological processes observed during treatment is the most certain portion of psychoanalysis and represents also the most detailed and reliable insight into human personality of which psychology is capable at the present time. I have tried to give a notion of this core of the psychoanalytic system as clearly and simply as is feasible, without sacrificing to simplicity the truthfulness of the picture. I hope that it will help to dissipate the hazy and inadequate notions which usually even well oriented physicians and laymen have of psychoanalysis. I hope also to have made clear that analytical therapy, as far as knowledge of the "therapeutic process" is concerned, is as well founded as therapy in organic medicine, and that a great part of medical therapy is even far behind analytical technique in its understanding of the curative processes.

The ideas developed in the chapter about "Psychogenic Factors" follow the lines of a series of lectures, which I gave at the University of Chicago in the years 1930–1931. The content of the first chapter was given January 15, 1931, as a Harvey Lecture in the New York Academy of Medicine. Several chapters have been published previously in the *Journal of the American Medical Association,* the *Archives for Neurology and Psychiatry,* and in the *American Journal of Orthopsychiatry.* Although some alterations have proved necessary, I am indebted to the various editors for permission to reprint. I wish, also, to thank Dr. Thomas French and Mr. Robert Casey for their kind revision of the manuscript.

F. A.

Boston, Mass.
November, 1931.

Preface to the Second Edition

SINCE this book was first published systematic clinical studies in the field of psychic influences on organic disturbances which my collaborators and I have conducted in the Chicago Institute for Psychoanalysis made possible a more definite formulation of certain assumptions and principles that were only tentatively treated in the first edition. This required extensive changes and additions. The fourth chapter of the first edition has been replaced by two new chapters with the titles of "Psychic Influences on Body Functions" and "Recognition of Psychic Factors in Modern Medicine." Moreover, another new chapter has been added: "The Sociological and Biological Orientation of Psychoanalysis," which had been in part published in *Mental Hygiene*. I wish to thank the editor for permission to reprint.

Because of the more general orientation of this book the detailed results of our clinical research work are not included. At this place I wish to express my gratitude to my collaborators, Doctors Catherine Bacon, Thomas M. French, Margaret Gerard, Edwin Eisler, Harry B. Levey, Maurice Levine, Helen V. McLean, Karl Menninger, William F. Menninger, George Mohr, Leon J. Saul, Lucia E. Tower, and George W. Wilson, whose systematic clinical studies contributed greatly to the development of the fundamental ideas treated in the two new chapters. I also wish to thank Mr. William T. Harrison for his help in preparing the index to the new edition.

F. A.

La Jolla, California
August, 1936.

I.

Psychoanalysis and Medicine

The Problematic Position of Psychoanalysis in Medicine

For about thirty years psychoanalysis, a theoretical concept of the personality, a precise and elaborately described method of psychological research and a therapy of mental disturbances, has been living a peculiarly isolated existence on the borderline of medicine and of the natural sciences. This borderline existence is not due entirely to the unreceptive attitude of medicine toward psychoanalysis, for psychoanalysis itself has also been undecided as to where it belongs. Many psychoanalysts, in fact, question whether psychoanalysis should not be considered a distinct discipline, related to medicine but essentially independent of it, just as archaeology, though related to history, is nevertheless itself a self-sufficient science, or as paleontology is related to geology but different in its methods and purpose. Even those psychoanalysts who, like myself, are convinced that, so far

as psychoanalysis is therapeutic, it belongs to medicine, cannot overlook the fact that its subject matter,
methods and terminology are so different from those
of medicine that its assimilation to it is extremely
difficult. Indeed, a clear decision on the citizenship
of this young empiric discipline in the realm of
science is theoretically as well as practically a highly
complicated and unsolved problem. Medicine aims
within certain limits to understand the body as a
physico-chemical machine; psychoanalysis deals with
psychological facts and tries to influence psychological
processes by psychological methods. Therefore, by
definition, psychoanalysis should be excluded from
medicine.

Mental processes, however, belong to the characteristic manifestations of biological systems and, as is
generally known, influence such physiological phenomena as weeping, blushing, respiration, or the secretion of the gastric juice. Furthermore, a number of
diseases manifest themselves in mental disturbances
such as psychoses and psychoneuroses. Even after the
cell-physiology of the brain has been highly developed
it is improbable that physiological or pharmacological
methods will be used to influence people's minds, for
example, to persuade someone or to explain a mathe-
matical thesis. In influencing pathological mental
processes, psychological methods are used which are

essentially similar to persuasion and explanation. Probably the best method of influencing disturbances of a psychological nature will always be through psychological means.

Nevertheless, to preserve the homogeneity of medicine, one might exclude psychological methods even though their scientific and therapeutic value were acknowledged, and regard psychology, pathopsychology and their practical application in psychotherapy as disciplines related to, but still lying outside of medicine. One must realize, however, that it is artificial to separate mental diseases from physical diseases, or mental processes from physical processes, for there is in reality a permanent interrelation between them. In therapy it is not always easy to decide in which cases a psychological and in which cases a physiological approach is indicated, for the individual cannot be divided into a body and a personality, since it is a psycho-biological entity.

Development of Psychoanalysis

Psychoanalysis started within medicine as an attempt to cure hysterical symptoms by psychological means. Under the influence of Charcot's studies on hysteria and its relation to hypnotic phenomena, Freud and Breuer developed the method of cathartic hypnosis. They observed that patients in hypnosis could remember certain forgotten events in their past lives which were intimately related to their symptoms. This recollection in hypnosis was accompanied by outbursts of emotion and usually followed by disappearance of the symptoms. This process of emotional abreaction in hypnosis Freud and Breuer called "catharsis" and their method "cathartic hypnosis." Freud, however, soon gave up the method of cathartic hypnosis and replaced it by the technique of free association. This technique supplied a more complete picture of the historical background of the symptoms and, apart from its therapeutic value, has yielded a deeper insight into human personality than was possible before. This method is responsible for the fact that psychoanalysis, two decades after it started as a modest therapeutic attempt to influence hysterical phenomena, has developed a consistent theory of the personality.

The fundamental concept of the unconscious has deeply influenced all modern thinking. The discovery of the far-reaching dynamic effect of unconscious mental processes on overt behavior, which has shown the limitations of the rational and conscious part of personality, has become so fundamental to the mental attitude of the educated man of the twentieth century that without it much of modern life is unintelligible. It is not an exaggeration to compare the change in attitude toward external reality which has resulted from this discovery with the change that the Copernican system effected four hundred years ago. The theory of the unconscious involves a new and definite break with the anthropocentric attitude toward the external world. The system of Copernicus destroyed anthropocentricity in the spatial cosmological sense, but man remained anthropocentric in a psychological sense. This becomes especially clear if we recall the doctrines of the rationalistic philosophers of the seventeenth and eighteenth centuries, who put all their faith and hope in the omnipotence of the thinking mind. Instead of the earth, the human mind became the center of the universe. This started with Descartes' teaching that nothing is certain except one's own thoughts, and this doctrine led in a direct line to Kant's consistently anthropocentric thesis: The external world, as we see it, is dependent on the mind and its categories, which are themselves absolute and belong to the unchangeable structure of the mind. Psychoanalysis as a genetic theory has dethroned these despots of philosophic thinking, the Kantian categories, and considers them as products of the adjustment to the physical environment. The infant's mental processes are subject neither to the logical nor to the moral categories of Kant and, what is more important, even in the adult's unconscious personality

there are mental processes which are not subject to
the laws of logic. These processes, manifest for example in dreams, do not follow the law of causality,
only that of temporal sequence, and are not bound by
such axioms as that the same thing cannot be at the
same time in two different places. Briefly, rational
thinking as well as moral feelings and prescriptions
are products of the adjustment of the organism to its
environment, but they do not entirely determine our
thinking and behavior, and a dynamically powerful
portion of mental life is neither rational, *i.e.* adjusted
to the external world, nor moral, *i.e.* adjusted to the
demands of the community. The rationally adjusted
part of the personality in everyone is in steady conflict
with the unadjusted layers. The means of eliminating
the disturbing influence of unadjusted tendencies is
a dynamic act called repression, by which the unadjusted mental forces are excluded from consciousness
and become unconscious. Thus, human personality
can be divided into two parts, the adjusted "ego" and
the original and impersonal "id," which is not yet
brought into a harmonious unity and which contains
different conflicting instinctual tendencies. In psy-
chopathic personalities this conflict between the
infantile and the adult portions of personality is quantitatively greater but qualitatively the same as in normal
individuals. Thus mental disturbances, such as psy-

choneuroses and psychoses, can be understood as more intensive and overt manifestations of the unadjusted unconscious parts of the personality.

All these concepts are today not only generally accepted but emotionally assimilated, and like the theory of evolution or the cosmological doctrine of the planetary systems have become an integral part of modern thinking. The emotional consequence of this modified perspective is that man now feels himself more definitely to be only a small part of the universe. Because his belief in the absoluteness of his rational thinking has been broken, even this last claim to a special position in the world has lost its foundation. Rational thinking can no longer be regarded as its own self-sufficient cause, unapproachable by further scientific research, but must be thought of as a product of adjustment to the world, and is not only not absolute, but is as relative as that birds fly and fishes swim. Our logical thinking is just as little the only possible form of thinking as flying is the only possible form of locomotion.

The scientific consequence of this new perspective is that psychology becomes relevant to biology. Thinking is one of the functions of the biological system, one means of orientation to the external world. The mental apparatus can be understood in the same way as the circulatory system, which in all its details is adjusted to the hydrodynamic problems which it has to solve. Similarly, the functions of the mental apparatus can be understood as adjustments to the problem of orientation to the environment. No teleologic philosophy is involved in this view.

Thus definitely separated from philosophy, psychoanalytic psychology becomes a mechanical, or better, a dynamic science and describes the functions of the mental apparatus in terms of mechanisms or dynamisms. It studies in detail the development of the mind in all its phases during the difficult process of adjustment, and follows the changes from the unorganized, unsystematic, diffused manifestations of the infant's mind into the complicated system of the adult ego. It explains pathological mental phenomena as due to the incomplete mastery of early unadjusted periods and it can determine, to a large extent, which phase of development was unsuccessfully passed through, or, in other words, to which phases of early development certain types of mentally disturbed individuals remain fixed.

This genetic and dynamic approach to the understanding of mental disturbances can be considered a decisive step in psychopathology. The psychodynamic approach makes possible the intelligent and systematic influencing of pathological mental processes, that is to say, a causally oriented psychotherapy.

Psychotic and neurotic symptoms can be understood on the basis of this conflict between the infantile remnants and the adult part of the personality. The chief difference between a neurosis and a psychosis is the extent to which the repressed unadjusted mental content breaks through into consciousness, after overcoming the resistance of the repressive forces. This breaking through of repressed content is much more complete in the different forms of psychoses. In the end-phases of schizophrenia, for example, one has the impression that the ego has given up all resistance and is dominated entirely by hallucinatory mental processes. In a psychosis even the very first adjustment of the ego breaks down, *i.e.,* the capacity to subordinate the satisfactions of imagination to the evidence of sense perceptions, and the consequence is a loss of orientation to the world. Of course, all the later achievements of development, such as esthetic and moral restrictions and inhibitions, also disappear in the psychosis. A psychosis can thus be considered as a flight from reality and, more particularly, from an adult form of existence back to childhood, to a happier time, in which phantasy prevails unhampered by actuality.

In the different forms of psychoneuroses the conflict between the two poles of personality, the conscious ego and the primitive id, is more obvious, since neither of them has a decisive victory. If the end-phases of a psychosis be compared with a silent battle-field after all the soldiers on the one side have been killed, a psychoneurosis is a battle still in progress, for psychoneurotic symptoms are partly manifestations of repressed tendencies and partly reactions of the ego against these tendencies. In psychoneuroses the conscious ego has still the upper hand, although it does not succeed entirely in repressing the unconscious tendencies. The important fact which shows the partial control of the ego is that the unconscious mental content can appear in consciousness only in distorted forms. These distortions are compromises between the two antagonistic forces in the mental apparatus; that is to say, they are a compromise between repressed and repressing forces. In these distorted forms the unconscious content can appear in consciousness without hurting the conscious personality.

Psychoneurosis and psychosis can be considered as different stages of the same mental process, the breaking through of the unconscious, repressed, primitive part of personality. In a psychosis the process goes much further, for the difference between conscious and unconscious disappears and the unconscious dominates the whole personality, whereas in a neurosis the principal achievement of the later ego-development, the acceptance of reality, remains more or less intact, and the unconscious tendencies penetrate the ego only in isolated symptoms, which play the rôle of foreign bodies embedded in normal tissue.

Apart from these results in the field of psychopathology, one type of dynamic manifestation of repressed mental force has a special significance for internal medicine: the so-called hysterical dysfunctions and organ-neuroses, in which unconscious psychic tendencies produce physical symptoms. The investigation of this field requires an intimate coöperation of internal medicine and psychoanalysis, and much must be left to the future.

All these discoveries of psychoanalysis in the field of mental pathology have become integral parts of modern medical thinking as the fundamental notions of the unconscious and repression have penetrated contemporary thought. The theory of fixation to infantile attitudes and the characteristic tendency of psychoneurotics and psychotics to regress to these early patterns of thinking and feeling belong today to the basic concepts of psychiatry. Furthermore, psychic mechanisms such as rationalization and projection, which have been understood as means of solving the conflict between the conscious ego and the wishes and tendencies unacceptable to it, are so generally accepted and employed not only in psychiatry, but even in general thought and conversation, that the young student of medicine often does not even know their origin in the psychodynamic system of Sigmund Freud.

In addition to the explanation of the apparently senseless mental processes of the psychoneurotic and insane, psychoanalysis has become the psychology of all kinds of irrational phenomena, such as casual slips and errors of everyday life, free-phantasy and especially dreams. It shows that the apparent irrationality of all these phenomena is due to the fact that our mature rational thinking has grown away from the more primitive stages represented in dream life. If, however, we relearn the primitive language of the mental life of our childhood, we are able to understand the psychological meaning of our dreams.

Resistance to Psychoanalysis

In what follows we shall concentrate our interest on those fundamental results of psychoanalytic psychology which have become or are becoming significant for medicine. These results are by no means of such a character that they explain the resistance offered to them, especially by the medical world. On the contrary, just this approach to the problems of mental life brings psychology nearer to biology and severs its traditional connection with philosophy.

As a matter of fact, the resistance to psychoanalysis is a complex phenomenon and has changed its nature during the thirty years since psychoanalysis began to affect the habits of thinking and feeling of the scientific world and the general public. Resistance was, at first, largely emotional and due to certain special results of the new empirical and microscopically detailed study of mental life. The discovery of infantile sexuality and of certain infantile, asocial and consequently repressed mental tendencies, which are present in everybody's unconscious, provoked general hostility. These first manifestations of resistance have been so often and so well described that there is no need to repeat them, especially as they have largely disappeared. In the last thirty years the world has changed a great deal in both its emotional and intellectual attitude, and to this change psychoanalysis has substantially contributed. This first, heroic period of psychoanalysis, in which it had to fight chiefly against emotional prejudices, is practically over. The Œdipus complex has found its acceptance in two most conservative places—in the Oxford dictionary and *Punch*. Psychoanalysts who still think that they have to awaken humanity from its indolent sleep are tilting with windmills.

Resistance has become gradually more intellectual. This intellectual resistance is based on inveterate

habits of thinking and established methods of investigation. It is no longer directed against the general or philosophic consequences of psychoanalysis
which have become generally assimilated into modern
thought and has, indeed, disappeared from all fields
except the birthplace of psychoanalysis: medical
research and therapy. Psychoanalysis no longer needs
to seek acceptance as a theory of personality but of
medicine, in spite of the fact that it is due to this new
dynamic point of view that psychiatry has advanced
beyond its merely descriptive stage and has become
an explanatory science.

Let us turn our attention now to this more serious
intellectual resistance which makes it so difficult for
the medical world to accept psychoanalysis.

I have referred already to the kernel of this resistance. Psychoanalysis deals with psychic phenomena
and so brings a new element into medicine. It introduces a subject matter which cannot be expressed in
terms of time and space and threatens to disturb the
homogeneity of medicine, which would prefer to deal
exclusively with physico-chemical facts and to employ
chiefly experimental methods. The subject matter as
well as the procedure of psychoanalysis is apt to arouse
the natural scientist's distrust of psychological facts
and methods. Thus the paradoxical situation has
arisen that psychiatry, an acknowledged part of medi-

cine, necessarily shares the fate of psychoanalysis and loses the respect of the rest of the medical world, since —especially here in America—it has assimilated so much from psychoanalysis.

The homogeneity of a science, the uniformity of the methods employed, are no doubt respectable postulates, but there are more important principles in scientific research. There *are* mental phenomena and they *are* interrelated with other biological phenomena, and science cannot close its eyes to phenomena only because it cannot master them with the usual tested methods. Subject matter is primary, not method, and the method must be adjusted to the nature of the subject matter. It is, however, a common tendency of the mind, a kind of inertia of thinking, to force methods that have proved successful in one field on a new but different field, instead of seeking for new and specially adjusted methods which the new field of phenomena requires. Had psychoanalysis been an experimental science, no resistance to it would have been offered by medicine. It would in this case probably have been accepted by medicine, but it would have had to abandon the investigation of the problems of personality. On the other hand, it is undeniable that distrust of psychological method was well founded. Although psychology has claimed to be a non-philosophic discipline since the middle of the last century, until Freud's appearance it could not produce results of an empirical nature adequate to dissipate the distrust against it. Until then there had been no prospect that psychology would ever be able to disavow the pessimistic statement of Moebius of the "hopelessness of every psychology."

The Nature of Psychological Understanding

Indeed, to understand the personality of another individual requires methods in many respects basically different from those employed in the natural sciences. Every empirical science consists in the refinement and systematic development of the methods of observation used in everyday life. In any science we can use only the senses we actually possess, although we can increase their exactness and eliminate to some degree their defects. Psychoanalysis, in contrast to earlier psychological methods, has simply refined and systematized the everyday methods used to understand other persons' mental situations. This common sense understanding is, however, a complex faculty. Its chief instrument is a kind of identification with the other person, that is, a putting of one's self in the other person's mental situation. If you observe the movements of another, the expression of his face, the tone of his voice, and if you listen also to what he says, you get an idea of what is going on in his mind. This understanding is derived from the fact that the object of observation is a being similar to the observer—both are human personalities. This similarity between observer and observed is quite essential and is found only in the field of psychology. If you observe physical phenomena, such as the behavior of two spheres which move on a table, you are entirely limited to what you see and are absolutely unable to foretell what will happen in the next moment unless you have learned the nature of such rolling spheres through previous experiences. If you observe another person, you note his external behavior, but you also know from your own introspective experience what you feel when you behave similarly and use the same facial expression, words, movements, as the observed person does. You understand the other person's motives because you know your own reaction in a similar situation. In psychological observation the external behavior of the observed object is supplemented by direct or introspective knowledge of one's own person.

The importance of this coexistence of objective and introspective observation in psychology cannot be stressed enough, not only because it is the basic difference between physical and psychological science but also because it is the only advantage of psychological observation over the physical research, which, on the other hand, has a great number of advantages,

the greatest of which is the possibility of experimentation. All psychological methods which fail to recognize and exploit this one advantage of psychological
examination must necessarily have a limited value
in the investigation of human personality. Experimental psychology and behaviorism have imitated
the methods of experimental science and have, therefore, either neglected to use and develop the natural
faculty of understanding other persons' mental
processes or, as in the case of behaviorism, have specifically refused to use this faculty. The pre-scientific
man interpreted even inanimate nature psychologically and saw the wrath of God behind thunder
and punishment behind lightning. Behavorism makes
exactly the opposite error and refuses to analyze the
psychic background even of living beings. Animism
attributed personality to inanimate nature, but behaviorism wishes to rob even human beings of their
personality. It is both an amusing and depressing
sight to observe how behaviorism stubbornly deprives
itself of one source of knowledge and restricts itself
to the observation of the so-called external behavior.
Are not words also objective facts, and when you hear
words how can you prevent them from conveying
knowledge of another's psychic processes?

I admit that this common sense understanding of
other individuals' mental situations is an unreliable

method. But is not the task of every science to improve on natural faculties of observation? Is not
unaided optical observation also unreliable? Was it
not necessary to add to it by scales and magnifying
pointers of physical instruments and microscopes?

Sources of Error in Psychological Observation

I think it is time now to describe more concretely
what I mean by the natural faculty of understanding
another person's mental condition.

You see a common soldier attack an officer and
ask him why he did it. He tells you how his superior
treated him unjustly for a long time and continually
humiliated him until finally he lost control of himself. Then you understand his position because everyone has experienced similar feelings. When you say,
therefore, that the soldier attacked his superior because the latter treated him unjustly and that finally
the soldier's embitterment became stronger than his
fear of punishment, you have a causal theory of his
behavior which contains even a plausible quantitative
judgment. As much understanding as this can be
attained by common sense, which is a natural faculty
comparable to our visual and acoustic faculties except
that it is much more complex. This faculty of psychological understanding employs the various forms of
sense perception and in addition the introspective

knowledge of one's own emotions which one uses through identification in the understanding of others. This faculty, which is possessed in varying degrees by everyone, is the basis of psychoanalysis, just as the optic and acoustic perceptions are the basis of physical experimentation. But science begins with the refinement and development of these everyday methods and faculties. It is obvious that common sense in psychology is a somewhat unreliable method. There are in it several sources of error. The *first* and most important is that—referring again to our simple example—the common soldier who tells you his story has no reason for telling you all his motives in attacking his superior. He will give you a story which puts him in a good light. You may, if you are an expert in human nature—what in Germany they call a good *Menschenkenner*—guess his real motives and discount his distortions, but you have no evidence as to whether you are right or not.

A *second* source of error is that even if the soldier wanted to describe to you the actual mental condition in which he acted he is unable to do so because he himself does not know all of his motives. He deceives not only you but also himself, and by his story he tries to put himself in a good light not only in your eyes but also in his own. In mentioning this second source of error, however, I am referring to one of the basic findings of psychoanalysis, that is, the fact of repression, which is a dynamic tendency to keep out of consciousness desires and motives which would disturb the harmony of the conscious ego and disturb the good opinion which we like to have of ourselves.

A *third* possibility of error is that the soldier may be so different from you in his psychological make-up that you cannot understand his motives. The possibility of identification is contingent on a similarity between observer and observed. This similarity always exists to some degree, since both observer and observed are human beings, but differences of sex, race, nationality, social class, and so forth, diminish this similarity and bring into play new sources of error. Men understand each other better than they do women, and women understand each other better than they do men. We understand people of a Western civilization better than we do Orientals. The greater the difference between two minds, the greater the difficulty in understanding.

The difficulties of adults in understanding either young children and savages or psychotics and neurotics have the same ground, *viz.*, that their mental processes are different from the mental processes of normal adults and belong to a more primitive level of mental development.

Finally, a *fourth* source of error is that the observer

himself has, as it were, psychological blind spots due
to his own repressions. He has motives which he excludes from his own consciousness and does not want
to admit even to himself and he will not, therefore,
be able to detect these in other persons. Again, one
requirement of psychological understanding, the introspective knowledge of one's own mind, is often
lacking in untrained observation because in certain
situations this introspective knowledge is blocked by
the repression of one's own motives. The dynamic
importance of one's own repressions as an obstacle in
understanding the mentality of others can be appreci-
ated only if we realize that the uniformity and harmony
of our conscious ego are guaranteed solely by these
repressions. To become an adult it is necessary to
forget the infantile way of thinking. The attraction
of this infantile form of mental life is great since it is
subject in a much higher degree to the pleasure
principle than adult mentality, which has had to adjust itself to reality. It is characteristic of infantile
mental life that it does not take into consideration
objective facts which resist subjective wishes and
needs. The recognition of a strange and by no means
always benign external reality is the problem which
the child has to solve in his later development. The
most important means of overcoming the infantile
form of thinking and infantile wishes and tendencies

is repression, through which the ego banishes the disturbing remnants of his infantile existence. Through repression these infantile remnants become unconscious and form the unconscious part of the personality. The special difficulty in understanding children, savages and the insane is thus based not only on the differences between their mentality and ours, but also on a mental force within ourselves which prevents us from understanding them—I mean repression. To be a normal adult, the primitive part of one's personality must be forgotten or rather overcome, and therefore the primitive mental processes of others and one's own dreams which are manifestations of an infantile personality are difficult to comprehend. In the investigation of mental pathology, science has to overcome the subjective difficulty inherent in the fact of repression.

I admit that the enumeration of the many sources of error which have been classified under these four categories is likely to encourage skepticism of the possibility of any scientific psychology. Some of these difficulties seem simply insurmountable and sufficiently explain why psychology failed for so long a time to find a method capable of eliminating or diminishing all these types of errors. Psychology, therefore, has not been a science, but the privilege of a few geniuses, the great *Menschenkenner,* authors, novelists and dramatists. Only these have been able to overcome, at least to some degree, most of the difficulties in understanding other persons' real motives in spite of the human tendency to deceive one's self as well as others, and in spite of the differences of age, race and sex. Geniuses are able to do this because the fourth source of error, their own repressions, is less developed than in others. Weak repressions are just what make some people better *Menschenkenner* than others, for in knowing their own personality, they are better able to understand others.

Elimination of the Sources of Error

Certain methodological discoveries have made it possible for psychology to become a science of personality. That every scientific development follows methodological discoveries and innovations is well known. Anatomy began with the introduction of dissection, histology with the miscroscope, bacteriology with methods of growing cultures. Psychology, as an empirical science of personality, began with the discovery of the method of free association by Freud.

I do not maintain that all four sources of error are entirely eliminated by the method of free association, but they are reduced to such a considerable degree that the requirements of an objective science are met. The patient is requested to report everything that occurs to him during the analytic session. He is asked to verbalize everything that occurs to him in the original sequence and form without any modification or omission. He is asked to assume a passive attitude toward his own trains of thought, in other words, to eliminate all conscious control over his mental processes to which he gives free rein and merely report them. This simple procedure seems at first to be a rather trivial device and it is not so easy to appreciate its value in research, but it is no less true that the methods of percussion and auscultation appear unpretentious and trivial, and it is only the interpretation of the small acoustic deviations that make them so important for medicine.

The first source of error, namely, the individual's lack of interest in giving a full account of his mental state, is eliminated in psychoanalysis by the fact that the subject is a patient. Only a sick and suffering person who hopes for a cure of his symptoms by following the physician's prescriptions will be willing to coöperate and give such an intimate insight into his personality as is required by the method of free association. In yielding to spontaneous trains of thought, ideas soon crop up which are usually put aside and forced from the focus of attention. While one yields to this uncontrolled manner of thinking in eliminating or at least diminishing the conscious control, an unknown part of the personality becomes manifest and all kinds of disagreeable and irrational notions and imagery appear which controlled thinking interrupts and blocks before they come to full clarity. In the analysis the patient gradually learns to overcome his natural reluctance to abandon the conventional façade which people habitually turn toward one another, and becomes entirely frank, displaying himself in a kind of mental nudity not only to the analyst but, what is equally novel, to himself. From this point of view it may be claimed that the patient's desire to be cured supplies an indispensable factor in an efficient psychological investigation, for it alone guarantees a willingness for unreserved self-revelation.

The only other situation which meets this requirement is a didactic analysis in which a student of analysis subjects himself to the procedure in order to learn the technique of analysis. In this case it is not the hope of being freed from disease but the wish to learn the method by studying one's self that guarantees frankness. Without coöperation between the observer and the observed, psychology is impossible. In physics, the willingness of inanimate objects to be studied is not necessary, but in psychology the analyst is absolutely dependent on this willingness.

The second source of error, namely, that the observed individual on account of his repressions is unable to give a full report of his own mental state, has also been solved by means of the analytic technique, which serves to eliminate the conscious control of mental processes. Spontaneous trains of thought are in a much higher degree subject to the repressed mental forces than ordinary thinking. Such trains of association are no longer determined by conscious processes and, therefore, display a more irrational character, similar to day-dreams or states of drowsiness. Long and patient observation of uncontrolled free associations has led to the development of a technique of interpretation that allows the psychoanalyst to reconstruct the unconscious tendencies which determine the sequence and content of these spontaneous trains of thought. In this way he is able to obtain a deeper insight into the make-up of the personality and to understand motives and emotional connections which are normally covered up by the controlling and selective functions of the conscious ego. Thus the second source of error, the inability of the patient to give a full account of his motives, is eliminated.

The third source of error was a subjective one, *viz.*, the difference between the observer and the observed. In some cases identification is almost impossible, as, for example, in the case of the mentally sick who revert to primitive infantile forms of mental activity. The length of an analysis, covering daily interviews over a period of months, is the only means by which this difficulty can be overcome. If you travel in a foreign country you are at first quite unable to understand the mentality of the inhabitants, even though you may understand their language. Their facial expressions and their reaction patterns are unfamiliar. But in time you learn their reactions without being able to tell how and why, and you gradually become able to orient yourself psychologically. The same thing happens in the course of a long psychoanalysis. Even a peculiar neurotic personality becomes familiar through prolonged and patient observation.

Finally, the fourth source of error, due to the blind spots of the observer caused by his own repressions, must also be eliminated, if psychoanalysis is to be regarded as a reliable form of investigation. The means of overcoming this difficulty is the preparation of the observer through his own analysis, in which he overcomes his repressions, learns to understand the unconscious part of his personality, and understands manifestations in others to which he was previously blind. I feel that I must explain this difficulty in a more concrete way by referring again to the example of the soldier who attacked his superior. Assume that the observer is a person of a basically tyrannical nature who, however, will not admit his tyrannical propensities even to himself and tries to explain away his own aggressive and domineering tendencies. Such a person, observing the scene between the soldier and his superior, will be inclined to overlook the superior's brutality or tyranny and will tend to blame the soldier for the officer's aggressions. He will have great difficulty in understanding the point of view of the common soldier and in justifying his resentment, and will tend to see in him a rebel and thus justify the attitude of the tyrannical officer, with whom he can more easily identify himself. He wants to keep his own tyrannical impulses concealed from himself and, at the same time, to give vent to them. He is, therefore, blind to similar tendencies in others, for in recognizing them he runs the danger of being forced to admit them in himself.

The didactic analysis which every trained analyst undergoes serves to overcome this subjective source of error. It increases the knowledge of the analyst's own personality and enables him to allow for the disturbing influence of his own character. The International Psychoanalytic Association has therefore for many years made it obligatory for every psychoanalyst to undergo an analysis himself before undertaking to analyze others. Just as astronomical observation must discount subjective error which is called the "personal equation," so psychoanalytic observation is impossible without knowing the peculiarities of one's own personality which may interfere with an objective psychological observation.

There are, therefore, four sources of error inherent in ordinary psychological observation which systematic psychoanalytic technique avoids in four ways: The unwillingness of the patient to disclose himself to the analyst is offset by his desire to be cured; the inability of the individual to give a full account of his mental state is overcome by the method of free association; the difference between observer and observed is made less effective by the long and systematically repeated observation; and the blind spots of the observer are helped by the didactic analysis. By these four devices, psychoanalysis has succeeded in refining the ordinary faculty of understanding the mental processes of others and in developing it into a scientific method which can be learned and controlled objectively by almost any serious student.

The efficiency of this method has been best proved by the fact that insight has been gained into cases in which ordinary understanding and even the genius of the great authors has entirely failed, the cases of psychosis and psychoneurosis. The seemingly unintelligible irrational and senseless behavior of the insane, the strangeness and irrationality of the psychoneurotic symptoms, can be psychologically explained and translated into intelligible language.

Psychoanalysis as a Therapeutic Method

The importance of the desire to be cured which, except for the didactic analysis, is the only effective condition for detailed psychological research, is responsible for a unique feature of psychoanalysis: I mean the coincidence of therapy and research. In psychoanalysis research takes place during the treatment, or, in other words, the methods of the treatment and research coincide.

After Freud had learned that neurotic symptoms are dynamic manifestations of repressed mental tendencies which the patient excludes from his consciousness and which return into consciousness in a disguised form as unintelligible symptoms, he realized that the way to free the patient from his symptoms was to make conscious the underlying repressed tendencies. In this way psychoanalysis extends the conscious ego's field of activity to portions of the personality which are unconscious before the treatment. The patient, as a result of the emotional experiences in the analysis, becomes more conscious of himself and more able to control his mental energies than before. He becomes able, also, to master those forces which were expressed in neurotic symptoms and to use them for normal activities. In this way he is cured. The aim of therapy and research is the same, a more complete knowledge of the personality; and this is unique in the field of medicine. In all other forms of medical treatment the patient plays a passive rôle. It is not only not necessary to initiate the patient into the details and mechanisms of his disease, but it would in most cases be disadvantageous to do so. In psychoanalysis, however, the patient's knowledge of the repressed mental contents for his symptoms evinced itself as *the* therapeutic agent. This fortunate coincidence of therapeutic method with that of scientific investigation is responsible for the fact that therapy is not only one approach to scientific knowledge but the very source of it.

The psychoanalytic technique which I have lauded as the great methodological invention which has made a science out of the research of personality and an etiologic treatment out of psychotherapy may appear too simple and trivial to be hailed as responsible for the development of a new science. It may be asked: What is the great novelty of psychoanalysis? It takes suitable subjects who are willing to offer a view of their personalities and gives them simple technical instructions on how to give up the conscious control of their trains of association. The method is simple as every scientific method is, and the secret of its efficiency is that it is adjusted exactly to the nature of the subject matter of the investigation. The modern development of scientific medicine is similarly the result of the simple, but very important, device of dissecting and investigating all details of the body, instead of merely speculating about it. The psychoanalyst listens in the same way as the anatomist looks, and this analogy goes really deeper than it may seem. Pre-anatomic medicine consisted in vague generalizations and speculative concepts similar to those of the pre-Freudian psychology. Psychologists spoke about emotions, will, ideas, perceptions and apperceptions, but were not interested in the actual details of the mental content. The introduction of dissection was not easy and encountered all the emotional prejudices that the dissection of personality has aroused in our own day. If one reads the writings of some of Freud's critics in Germany and replaces the word "personality" or "mind" by the word "body," the same arguments which were advanced against the dissection of the body in the sixteenth and seventeenth centuries reappear. Psychoanalysis is a sacrilege, it degrades the mind, it drags down into the mud our highest mental possessions. One easily recognizes in these sentences the style of those who opposed dissection of the body. Anatomy and physiology caused great disillusionment, for scientists did not find any place for the spirit. Psychoanalysis has also caused disillusionment. The dissection of the mind reduces the complexity of personality with all of its highest strivings and intimate vibrations to a system of dynamic forces to which, from the scientific viewpoint, the categories of good and evil, high and low, beautiful and hideous, are inapplicable, though they naturally retain their significance in practical life.

I would give a false impression if I stressed only the simplicity of the psychoanalytic method. It is simple only in its general principle—that one has to listen to what the patient says. The scientific estimate of the material, however, is by no means simple. An elaborate technique of interpretation, based on long and painstaking comparisons, makes the learning of this method just as difficult as the use of the microscope. It requires long experience and a training of the complex faculty of understanding the mentality of others. Training in the method of interpretation itself can be compared with learning a new language. Dreams and all other manifestations of the unconscious mind speak a different language from that of the conscious mind. It is a language of pictures and its relation to conscious thinking is similar to the relation of ancient picture writing to modern alphabets.

Conclusions

I see the significance of psychoanalysis for medicine in the following two accomplishments: 1. With the help of a technique specifically adapted to the nature of psychic phenomena, it has developed a consistent and empirically founded theory of the personality, fit to serve as a basis for the understanding and treatment of mental disturbances. 2. It has given a concrete content to the philosophic postulate that living beings are psycho-biological entities, by investigating in detail the interrelation of physiological and psychological processes. The greater part of these investigations must, however, be left to the future for completion.

II.

The Present Status of Psychoanalysis
as a Theoretical and Therapeutic System

In the last three hundred years, several wholly new sciences have been created. Modern chemistry is hardly two hundred years old, and experimental biology and scientific medicine considerably less. The development of psychoanalysis in the last forty years from a special therapeutic device to a science of personality, with well defined and established methods of research is, therefore, an unusual cultural phenomenon. It is no wonder that in this short period the scientific world has not yet had time to assimilate this youngest of the scientific disciplines. Its relative novelty explains the widely different estimates recently made of it, some maintaining that it is one of the most important products of modern thinking, others wholly denying its scientific nature and prophesying its speedy disappearance.

How the first groping therapeutic attempts of Freud

and Breuer developed into a consistent and empirical theory of personality is itself a fascinating question which deserves to be investigated. It is, however, not unusual in the history of sciences as of other human endeavor that they lead to quite other than the expected results. I do not need to give examples of this in this continent, the very discovery of which is a classical example of such an unexpected result. The unexpectedly discovered territory in psychoanalysis is the knowledge of the structure of human personality.

The Theory of the Cathartic Hypnosis

The richness of theoretical results yielded by the psychoanalytic treatment of psychoneurotics is explained by the fact that in psychoanalysis the method of therapy and research is the same. Even when Freud still used the method of cathartic hypnosis, the reconstruction of the history of neurotic symptoms was the crucial element in therapy. Freud stated this fact in one of his very early writings in the formula that the psychoneurotic patient is suffering from reminiscences. The first result of observation of the mechanism of symptom-formation was that in hypnosis patients were able to remember certain events in their lives which they had entirely forgotten. This recollection in hypnosis, however, was not simple recollection, but a dramatic repetition of forgotten situations. These pathogenetic situations had been forgotten on account of their overwhelming nature. Freud and Breuer called such experiences "traumatic situations." A characteristic feature of such traumatic situations is that the patient cannot give expression to certain emotions. The dramatically expressed emotions which became manifest in hypnosis were just those which the patient had repressed in the traumatic situation. The first theoretical formulation of this was that the neurotic symptom is the dynamic equivalent of those emotions which had not been adequately expressed at the time when they arose. After these forgotten events had been remembered and the accompanying emotions found abreaction in hypnosis, the symptoms disappeared. They disappeared because they had lost their dynamic foundation. Freud's second logical, really inevitable, conclusion was that the reappearance of such forgotten emotional situations in hypnosis is due to the elimination of consciousness during hypnosis, so that the dynamic force responsible for the forgetting of certain experiences must be inherent in the particular state of consciousness. Freud expressed his conclusions in the following way: In certain situations—the so-called traumatic situations—the psychoneurotic patient was unable to face certain unbearable emotions and was forced to exclude them from his consciousness. These emotions, excluded from consciousness, found no adequate expression and relief and so maintained a permanent tension in the personality which the psychoneurotic symptoms are an attempt to relieve.

Another assumption made by this theory and well established by everyday observation was that every emotion has the tendency to be released by certain motor innervations, such as weeping, laughter, gestures, facial expression and more especially by their expression in speech. These reliefs are evidently possible only if the emotion is conscious; so that excluded from consciousness it is at the same time deprived of its normal and adequate expression. Hysterical symptoms are, according to this view, unusual motor innervations produced by unconscious, *i.e.* repressed wishes, which because of being repressed are excluded from normal expression. They have a definite psychological meaning, since they give symbolic expression to repressed but emotionally charged ideas and wishful phantasies (or their rejection).

Later, Freud, and more especially his follower, Ferenczi, drew the bold conclusion, again based on detailed observation, that practically all parts and functions of the body can be used to express emotion. The use of the striated muscles of the face and extremities is only one special case in which an idea or an emotion influences the function of organs. Theoretically, however, all organs can be used to express emotions or to release psychic tension. The anatomical and physiological basis of these innervations is well established. Through the peripheral and vegetative nervous system all portions of the body are directly or indirectly connected with the cortex. Psychogenic disturbances of the stomach or heart are no more mystical than the stimulation of the lachrymal sac by melancholy thoughts.[1]

Hysterical symptoms, in the light of these views, are unusual expressions of mental tensions, unusual because the organs influenced are, as a rule, not used for emotional expression or, at least, not in the same way. A close investigation has even shown that the organic expressions which at first seemed unusual are not so exceptional, nor are they present only in pathological cases, but that under the influence of a strong emotion, like fear, the heart, the blood vessels, the peristaltic movement of the intestines, the secretion of the skin glands, and the constrictor pupillae, all participate.

The only peculiarity of hysterical innervation is not the mere occurrence of unusual emotional expres-

[1] See the critical discussion of this extension of the theory of conversion hysteria on pages 191 to 198.

sions, but their permanency and the apparent absence of the accompanying emotion. Thus the only logical conclusion that could be drawn was that emotions excluded from consciousness are likely to create a permanent tension, and as a result of this tension, to occasion permanent or at least recurring disturbances of certain organ functions. In hysteria the underlying emotion disappears and gives place to its dynamic substitute, the symptom. The therapeutic idea was that if these repressed emotions could be brought to natural expression, they would cease seeking unusual outlet in pathological innervations of the organs. The natural expression of emotion is possible only through consciousness, so that the goal of therapy became the attempt to bring into consciousness repressed mental material.

Here can be seen the first point at which therapy and research converge. Psychological research aims to discover psychological connections and attempts to understand the psychological make-up of the personality, and the aim of psychoanalytic therapy is similarly to bring into consciousness unconscious mental connections, by increasing the patient's insight into his own mental processes. Thus even at the beginning of his psychotherapeutic work, during the period of coöperation with Breuer, Freud recognized that hysteria can only be cured by knowledge, and not by the physician's alone, but by the patient's knowledge of his own personality. This was the first step, historically, toward this unique mode of therapy, in which the cure is based upon the patient's knowledge of himself.

At the time, however, when the method of cathartic hypnosis was in use, this principle of bringing into consciousness unconscious material was not yet at all effectively realized, for the recollections of which the patient is capable under hypnosis do not belong to his conscious mental possessions. On awaking from hypnosis he is usually unaware of what has happened during the hypnosis. Such hypnotic recollection does not eliminate the cause of amnesia, *viz.*, the resistance of the conscious personality to facing the unbearable material which has been repressed. Furthermore, experience has shown that the abreaction of emotions during hypnosis does not result, in most cases, in a permanent cure; it means rather a temporary relief from accumulated and repressed mental tension. As long as the conscious personality is not able to face the repressed tendencies, the same emotional setting again becomes repressed and likely to produce new hysterical dysfunctions. Hypnosis can be considered as an ingenious trick which, by excluding the conscious personality, circumvents its resistance against certain repressed material. It is easy to understand that the next logical step must have been the attempt not to circumvent but actually to overcome the resistance of the conscious personality against the repressed material, to induce the personality to face the tendencies previously excluded from consciousness which are the dynamic cause of the symptoms.

At the time when Freud began his experiments in substituting another psychotherapeutic method for hypnosis, all these notions were not clearly formulated. It was by no means mere logic which led Freud to find another method, but his own creative genius. It is hard to reconstruct precisely all the motives which induced him to give up hypnotic treatment and I do not think that even he is able fully to account for it. The reasons stated in his writings do not appear entirely satisfactory. One reason that not every patient is susceptible to hypnosis is without doubt decisive, but also other more theoretical considerations must have influenced him to experiment with other methods. It soon became evident that the forgotten "traumatic" experience was not, in many cases, such a violent or extraordinary event as could have explained its pathogenic significance, so that the objective nature of the traumatic experience was by no means sufficient to explain its effect. Hypnotic experiments often revealed situations which seemed entirely harmless. For example, the famous patient of Breuer, on whom the very first cathartic observations were made, suffered among many other symptoms from hydrophobia. She would not drink water, but would quench her thirst only with melons and other fruits. During the hypnotic treatment one day she began to talk about her English governess whom she disliked very much and remembered that once, on entering the governess' room, a little dog was drinking water from a glass. Out of politeness, she suppressed her anger and did not say anything, but during the hypnotic session she was able both to remember the scene and to express the annoyance which at the time she had kept back. After giving full vent to her hostility to the governess, she asked for water and drank a good deal of it.

It is evident that the traumatic effect of this little scene in which the patient's hydrophobia had originated cannot be explained by the nature of the scene itself. The mere sight of a dog drinking out of a glass, without assuming a special sensitiveness of the patient to the scene, cannot explain its pathogenic effect. Evidently the symptom must have had some kind of historical background, and there must have been other earlier experiences which made the patient peculiarly responsive to this intrinsically harmless situation. As a matter of fact, neither Freud nor Breuer drew this conclusion clearly at the time of their coöperation, for traditional views of the French neurological school hindered their perception. In the beginning they accepted Charcot's vague concept of a special mental situation which he called "condition seconde" or "hypnoid" as responsible for the traumatic effect of certain situations. According to this theory some patients under violent emotions were apt to fall into peculiar states of split consciousness (hypnoid), in which they were especially sensitive to traumatic experiences, even if these were not especially violent, nor capable of exerting any effect on normal persons. This pathological inclination for falling into hypnoid states Freud and Breuer, at the beginning following Charcot's theory, ascribed to hereditary factors. Freud, however, never was really satisfied with this rather dogmatic explanation. In seeking a more satisfactory explanation, he observed that in hypnosis the violent abreactions of emotions during the recollection of traumatic situations were frequently not followed by a disappearance of the symptom. More hypnotic sessions were necessary in which other traumatic experiences of an earlier date came to abreaction. The symptom was not determined, as was assumed at the beginning, by *one* but by a whole chain of experiences, which regularly went back to puberty and quite monotonously had some connection with the sexual experiences or emotions of adolescence. It became evident that every symptom had a long and complicated historical background, and that hypnosis could only reveal a limited section of the past and did not give a complete picture of the patient's history. This conclusion furnished another motive which stimulated Freud to try other methods.

The problem which Freud faced at this stage was to force the patient to remember traumatic and consequently forgotten periods of his life without the exclusion of consciousness in hypnosis. Under the influence of Lieubeault's and Bernheim's experiments on suggestion in waking states, Freud tried to force his patients by means of suggestion to recall traumatic events in their lives. These suggestions, however, were no longer made in hypnosis, but to the fully conscious patient.

The Discovery of the Method of Free Association

After a short period of experiments with suggestion between 1890 and 1895, Freud definitely gave up hypnosis and suggestion and discovered the method of free association.

Whereas hypnosis and suggestion can be regarded as a frontal attack against the patient's resistance to letting repressed mental content enter consciousness, the new technique can be compared to a flank attack.

In this method the significant factor is the self-betray-ing tendency of the unconscious material, which seeks expression but is inhibited by repressing counter-forces. Once the patient abandons the conscious con-trol and direction of his ideas, the train of the free spontaneous associations is guided more by the re-pressed material than by conscious motives. The com-plete elimination of consciousness effected in hypnosis was replaced in this method by partial elimination, which dispenses only with the controlling forces of conscious personality.

This technique threw a new light on the origin of symptoms. It now became evident that the traumatic experience was only a precipitating factor and that it derived its traumatic quality from earlier experience. The new method was able to penetrate further, into the early infantile period, and proved that the trau-matic experiences of later life derived their traumatic quality from their intimate connection with similar emotional situations in early childhood. The uncon-trolled trains of thought revealed to the observer a fascinating interplay of two dynamic tendencies: to *express* and to *repress* some mental content of which the patient was unaware. This double tendency to express and conceal: the impulse to remember and confess something accompanied by the opposed in-clination to keep the same material out of consciousness, resulted in sequences of associations which led the observer to suspect covert allusions to a hidden content which the associations now approached, now avoided. This free association when extended over a sufficiently long period brought the patient back to forgotten periods of his life. Sometimes it resulted in the recollection of forgotten events as was the case in hypnosis, but even in the cases where distinct recollections were not abundant, the trains of association by increasingly clear allusions permitted a reliable reconstruction of the forgotten phases of the past. More important than this reconstruction of events was the fact that during the process of free association the unconscious emotions and tendencies which had been repressed at certain times in the past came to the surface. The emotional abreaction in free association is essentially similar to the abreaction under hypnosis, the only difference being that under hypnosis it is like an explosion concentrated in a short time, while in free association it extends over a long period. The same amount of emotion which comes to abreaction in a few minutes under hypnosis is dispersed in free associations over many months. The advantage of protracted emotional abreaction is that the patient's conscious ego is much better able to digest these emotions and to relate them with the rest of the mental life. This synthetic process of "working up" repressed emotions, which is a kind of mental digestion, is the most valuable therapeutic factor, because it means a permanent change in the total personality. The hypnotic abreaction was a kind of explosion in a state when consciousness was eliminated so that the principal aim of therapy, to make the patient able to face and to control these emotions, could not be realized.

With the introduction of this new method, psychoanalytic treatment became the coöperation between physician and patient in extending the activity of the conscious personality to such parts of the mental apparatus as had previously been unconscious. The chief practical and theoretical problem was concentrated in the attempt to find the causes of repression. Only after these were known was it possible to proceed deliberately to change the personality in a way to make repression superfluous. Here again a problem in therapy stimulated research into the dynamic structure of personality, and psychoanalytic theory and therapy in traditionally intimate connection were directed toward the understanding and overcoming of repressions. In order to give a clear picture of the later development of psychoanalysis, I must summarize briefly the first theoretical formulations of the experiences gained with the method of free association.

The Theory of Repression

The human personality is not a homogeneous entity; the conscious mental processes are only a part of the mental life, for there are also unconscious mental processes which are excluded from consciousness. The first assumption was that the mental content excluded from consciousness was of a kind the recognition of which would cause an unbearable conflict. In other words, everything contradictory to the ruling tendencies of the conscious personality, to its wishes, longings and ideals, and everything which could disturb the good opinion one likes to have of oneself is apt to be repressed. The homogeneity of the entity which we call and feel our actual ego is due to the dynamic fact of repression which excludes everything disturbing the harmony of this conscious part of the total personality. The first fundamental concept was a *topic,* and at the same time a *dynamic* one, the distinction between the conscious ego and the unconscious.

The second important discovery was that repression, though able to prevent some mental forces from becoming conscious, does not destroy the dynamic power of these repressed tendencies. On the contrary, the unconscious tendencies are able to influence overt behavior and at the same time to find special outlets in neurotic and psychotic symptoms and, more mildly, in common mistakes of speech and behavior, in dreams and day-dreams, in which repressed tendencies return to consciousness in a distorted form. Even the conscious and apparently rational behavior of normal persons is, to a certain degree, influenced by rationalized unconscious motives. Thus rational motives are often invented for behavior which is fundamentally determined by unconscious motives. The difference between normality and neurosis is only a quantitative difference in the extent to which unconscious tendencies dominate and determine behavior. Neurotic symptoms are eruptions of repressed tendencies, a kind of revolution of the repressed parts of personality which, in neurotics, apparently have a greater intensity. This notion conveys the uncanny impression that everyone is walking on the volcano of his unconscious personality, a statement which tries the conceited twentieth century which has placed so high an estimate on the sovereignty of the rational ego and furnishes a new reason for turning aside from the unpleasant truth discovered by psychoanalysis.

The Discovery of Infantile Sexuality

On investigating the conditions of repression, the first striking fact was the particular sensitiveness of the conscious ego to certain sexual tendencies. Investigation uncovered a most exciting drama in the depths of the personality—a drama in which civilized man is peculiarly involved—and in which the principal rôles are taken by the original biological impulse for the preservation of the race and the social restrictions placed by society upon this impulse. While the instinct for self-preservation is involved chiefly in conflict with external reality, the sexual instinct, as a consequence of social development, has to fight against inner restrictions within the personality. Once his interest was focused upon this typical repression of the sexual instinct, Freud made the discovery which immediately aroused general prejudice and animosity, *viz.*, the discovery of infantile sexuality.

Without knowledge of repression it is entirely impossible to understand how mankind was able to achieve this masterpiece of blindness and self-deception in overlooking the overt sexuality of the infant. Freud was indeed justified in appreciating so highly the observations of the Hungarian pediatrist, Lindner, who—a singular phenomenon—as early as 1879 recognized the sexual nature of the new-born infant's thumb-sucking. In the last thirty years, the sexual manifestations of the child have become a field for the most diligent observation, and many of the former opponents of infantile sexuality are today busy describing new sexual manifestations in the child.

Freud, however, was led to the discovery of infantile sexuality in a more indirect way. Having introduced the method of free association, he made the unexpected observation that neurotic patients following their spontaneous trains of thought for a sufficient length of time were led with astonishing regularity to early experiences of a distinctly sexual nature. The first theoretical estimate of this observation, however, was shown later to be erroneous. In the majority of cases, this early sexuality reflected in the patient's memories proved to be typical phantasies of childhood rather than real events and experiences. The notorious theory of the "infantile sexual trauma" had to be abandoned, and Freud in this case, as in many others, was free to admit his error and revise his older views. The fact which remained valid was that the child already in the very earliest period of his life is involved in certain typical emotions of a sexual nature which his personality is not able to face and relieve. Thus the theory of the early sexual trauma, although erroneous, led to a knowledge of early emotional conflicts of the child by calling attention to his early instinctual life.

The next fundamental statement which Freud made was that the repressions of most importance for later development must have grown out of the emotional conflicts of early childhood. It cannot be denied that, in the explanation of these early repressions, Freud at first one-sidedly emphasized the early sexual striving of the child, although in the detection of the Œdipus complex he recognized the basic importance of hostile tendencies directed against the parent of the same sex. The full theoretical appreciation of the significance of these hostile or destructive tendencies, however, came much later, owing to the fact that the theory of the instincts has always been the most speculative part of the psychoanalytical theory and consequently subject to the greatest changes.

The Theory of Instincts

The early distinction between the sexual libido and the instinct for self-preservation—also called "ego-instinct"—was merely descriptive, comparable to the first notions of electricity and gravity, which were not concerned with the ultimate nature of the force involved but merely tried to describe its manifestations. The distinction between the instinct for self-preservation and the sexual instinct, however, proved insufficient to give a theoretical explanation of the observed facts.

In its earliest manifestations in *oral* and *anal* eroticism, the libido is intimately connected with the functions of nutrition and excretion, which are usually considered manifestations of the instinct for self-preservation. But even in its sublime manifestation in love, the libido at an early period takes its own person as an object in a kind of self-love which Freud called "Narcissism." Only later, after the individual's system is fully saturated with libido, does the differentiation between the aims of self-preservation and those of race-preservation take place and the libido fasten upon others as objects of its attachment.[1] Even in adult life, however, the sexual life may regress in perversions to its early pregenital modes of expression.

It should be clear from this survey that at first there was little room in Freud's theory of instincts for the destructive instinctual tendencies. Broadly speaking, hatred and destruction were considered as manifestations of the instinct for self-preservation, also called ego-instinct, which was supposed to be connected with erotic factors in the form of sadism. Up to 1920 the libido-theory retained this looseness of expression

[1] Bernard Shaw, in his *Heartbreak House*, expresses the libido theory, the concept of Narcissism, and sublimation in a simple and convincing way. The coincidence between the Freudian concept and Shaw's philosophy, which he gives in the words of Captain Shotover, is remarkable.

Captain Shotover says: "A man's interest in the world is only the overflow from his interest in himself. When you are a child your vessel is not yet full; so you care for nothing but your own affairs. When you grow up, your vessel overflows; and you are a politician, a philosopher, or an explorer and adventurer. In old age the vessel dries up: there is no overflow: you are a child again."

and not until 1920 did Freud clarify the matter by distinguishing between two basic biological instincts —the *erotic* and the *destructive*. According to this theory, the erotic drive is a binding force with a tendency to build up higher biological systems, and its fundamental manifestation is the anabolic process of metabolism. The destructive tendency, on the contrary, is a separating force expressed biologically in the chemical process of katabolism. In agreement with biological ideas, Freud assumed that in their psychological manifestations these two tendencies were always mixed. The actually observed psychological processes are supposed to result from the mixture in varying proportions of these two basic tendencies. This concept, although unquestionably highly speculative, is in better accord with the observed facts than the old distinction between ego-instinct and sexual instinct, which was not able to describe and differentiate clearly enough a group of mental antagonists such as love and hatred and the creative and destructive strivings. The older distinction between self-preservative and race-preservative tendencies described not so much different qualities of two separate instincts as manifestations of the same mental force directed toward different objects. The erotic instinct in its narcissistic expressions has a function in self-preservation and, when directed against objects, in race-preservation. The distinction between the destructive and erotic tendencies, however, is a distinction of the basic qualities of the instincts. Such a distinction was necessary to describe such fundamentally different psychological phenomena as love and hate, or the biological opposites, reproduction and death.[1]

The Œdipus Complex

We may now disregard in what follows these speculative and by no means rigid or necessarily complete views as to the nature and qualities of the instincts. The statement of fact about the early emotional conflicts of the child have been fully corroborated by further research. Detailed observations have monotonously revealed that psychoneurotic patients remain involved in a strange way throughout their lives in a characteristic struggle between love, jealousy, the sense of inferiority, and a guilty conscience which begins in the Œdipus situation of early childhood. Freud explained the typical amnesia which covers the first six years and only permits isolated and apparently quite insignificant and fragmentary recol-

[1] In his theory of instincts Freud assumes that the destructive instinct is primarily directed against the organism itself and calls it also "death-instinct." This assumption has been questioned by many authors, whereas the distinction between erotic and destructive tendencies is a descriptive statement and has been generally accepted.

lections to survive as the result of strong repressions during these early years. These repressions are due to the discrepancy between the intensity of the emotions and the strength of the infantile ego. The infantile ego is not able to assimilate—one might even say digest—the emotions of love and jealousy, and can neither control nor renounce them, so that the only way left to solve these emotional conflicts is repression, *i.e.,* their elimination from the fields of consciousness. A peculiar anachronism is responsible for this discrepancy. The development of the instincts does not run parallel either with mental or genital growth. The child's personality has to face both psycho-sexual tension and aggressive impulses which his mind can neither control nor relieve by genital and muscular activity. This uneven development of the instinctual life on the one hand, and of intellectual and genital capacity on the other, is in the last analysis the basis of the child's emotional conflicts. Childhood is, consequently, the most vulnerable phase of human development. Mistaken educational principles, traumatic experiences of every kind which are apt to increase this conflict, may exert a pathogenic influence upon the whole later life.

After the pathogenic significance of the emotional conflicts of childhood had been corroborated by a vast amount of observation, the dynamic concept of repression could be completed by description of the kind of psychological content which was regularly repressed. Feelings of love and hate in the form of jealousy and in the specific relations in which they occur in family life undergo repression, and the infantile repressions form the pattern which, like a conditioned reflex, determines the repressions in later life.

Development of the Ego-Psychology

The structural and dynamic approach to the actually observed mental processes has in the last fifteen years undergone a rapid development. From 1921 on we can speak of the evolution of a new analytic ego-psychology. A deeper investigation of the fundamental processes of repression was the starting point of this new development. The central problem became: which psychic factors are responsible for repression and how does this process take place in detail? It soon became evident that fear is the motive power behind all repression. Characteristic of this fear, however, is the fact that it is by no means a rational or entirely conscious fear of external and actual danger but an inner fear which appears in consciousness as a guilty conscience. This phenomenon is most satisfactorily described by saying that one part of the personality exhibits fear of another part, which in ordinary language is called conscience, and that repression serves to avert this fear-reaction. In other words, those mental tendencies, wishes, longings, ideas, that would arouse self-condemnation if they entered consciousness are excluded from the conscious personality, for this self-condemnation is associated with fear similar to that experienced in the face of real danger. The historical investigation of the repressed tendencies has shown that those are apt to arouse a guilt-conflict which at some previous time, usually in infancy, had actually caused the individual pain, parental punishment or contempt. The fear of the parents thus becomes embodied in the fear of one's own conscience. The assumption was inevitable that during development a part of the personality assumes the attitude, opinions, and judgments of persons in authority, usually of the parents, and this embodiment of the parents now assumes the same attitude toward the rest of the personality as the parents previously manifested toward the child. This process of identification with the parents and the incorporation of their image into the mental apparatus is the process which we usually call adjustment to the social environment. One part of the personality accepts the code of education and becomes a representative of demands of society, and this part Freud called the *super-ego*. It is important to realize that not the whole of the personality participates in social adjustment and that even in normal persons there is a steady and permanent tension between the original, nonadjusted, instinctual tendencies, and the restrictive influence of the super-ego.

The existence of the super-ego explains how in every form of civilization there is a self-regulating or self-restrictive force in individuals which is indispensable for social order. If an internal code of law such as the super-ego or, to use the more popular expression, the conscience, were not present, social order could only be secured by assigning to every citizen a policeman to make him conform with accepted social behavior. Social behavior is by no means enforced only by fear of external punishment; there is also in every adjusted individual a restrictive force, which in the course of development becomes more or less independent of external reinforcement, such as admonition and threats of punishment. On the other hand, it also became evident in the light of psychological analysis that the inner assimilation of social prescriptions is limited to only a few, very fundamental regulations. Without the fear of punishment, the majority of people would behave less socially than they actually do, for the super-ego does not entirely replace real persons in authority.

The only way to test empirically which non-social tendencies are controlled by the internal restricting

functions of the super-ego and those which must still
be controlled by a police force, would be to make the
impossible experiment of abolishing all punishments.
A statistical investigation as to what kinds of crime
and unsocial behavior increase under these circumstances and what criminal tendencies no longer need
external control would furnish a criterion of the degree to which the man of today is essentially adjusted
to the requirements of collective life. From psychoanalytic experience it could be predicted with some
degree of probability that in our present civilization
only cannibalism, actual incest, parricide and fratri-
cide would not increase, even if there were no punishment for these crimes in the penal code. These non-
social tendencies, though manifest at the beginning of
man's development, are repressed in contemporary
civilization so successfully that there is no danger of
their actual realization. Cannibalism, for example, no
longer needs the special prohibitions necessary in
some primitive civilizations, for it is deeply repressed
although unquestionably existent at the beginning of
everyone's development.

Whereas the normal individual is able to domesti-
cate and modify his unsocial, instinctual tendencies,
the psychoneurotic remains more firmly fixated to
them. The way which the neurotic chooses for the
solution of his conflict between repressing and re-

pressed non-adjusted mental forces is a substitution of phantasy for the actual realization of his wishes, though not even in his phantasy can he express directly his non-adjusted tendencies, since the conscious, adjusted portion of his personality denies their existence. The outcome is a disguised phantastic expression of them in psychoneurotic symptoms.

Furthermore, the investigation of dreams has shown that even in normal persons unconscious remnants of non-social tendencies are at work, for the often unintelligible and senseless dreams of adults are disguised expressions of tendencies rejected by the adjusted part of the personality. Consequently dreams can be considered the neurotic symptoms of normal persons. In any case the dynamic basis of dream-formation is identical with that of neurotic symptom-formation and, in fact, the technique of dream analysis has proven to be the most delicate instrument for the investigation of the dynamic interplay of repressed and repressing mental forces. This microscopic research into symptom- and dream-formation has led to a kind of stereo-psychology, for it has developed a concept of the structure of personality and has reconstructed intrapsychic processes which go on between the structurally differentiated parts of the personality. We can distinguish three structurally differentiated parts of the mental apparatus:

(1) The inherited reservoir of chaotic, instinctual demands which are not yet in harmony with each other nor with the facts of external reality is called,

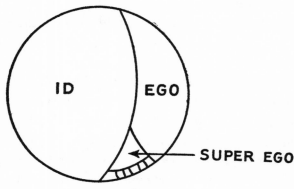

FIG. 1

The shaded portion of the section, which represents the super-ego, expresses the fact that the super-ego in a fully developed personality has lost its connection with external reality. It is more or less rigid and has sunk to the depth of the personality. It is consequently to a high degree unconscious.[1]

on account of its impersonal quality, the *id*. (2) The *ego* is the integrating part of the personality which modifies and, by a process of selection and control, brings the original tendencies of the id into harmony, excluding those the realization of which would occasion conflict with external reality. (3) Finally, the third part of the mental apparatus, the result of the

[1] In my book, *The Psychoanalysis of the Total Personality*, I proposed a distinction between the entirely unconscious super-ego and the conscious ego-ideal. The latter contains those specific values acquired in later life and which are the conscious directing forces

latest adjustment, is the *super-ego* which embodies the code of society. Naturally this code is dependent upon the social environment and differs according to the cultural milieu in which the individual was brought up.

It may sound paradoxical that our knowledge of the conscious ego is far behind what we know about the nature and functions of the id, and especially of the super-ego. It sounds paradoxical because the ego

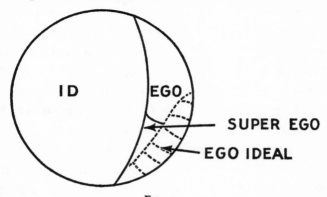

FIG. 2

The dotted line expresses the fact that the ego-ideal is not a completely separate unit, since it is hard to differentiate between conscious values, ideals, guiding principles and the rest of the ego. On the other hand, it is also difficult to make a sharp distinction between the entirely unconscious, almost automatic influences of the super-ego and those more or less conscious ones which direct our decisions and general conduct.

of conduct. This distinction was accepted by many psychoanalysts, but it seems to me questionable whether one should consider the ego-ideal more closely connected with the super-ego, as its continuation in the consciousness, or more allied to the actual ego. This could be expressed by the following diagram:

is the part of personality of which we are constantly aware and is the part which we think we know and feel as our actual personality. Perhaps, however, just this nearness to it is one of the reasons which makes its scientific investigation so difficult. The difficulty of understanding the ego with the help of the ego was expressed in older philosophical treatises by such metaphors as "it is impossible to cut a knife with a knife." Psychoanalysis, however, is not an introspective method, although it has to utilize introspection in understanding the personalities of others, because in psychology the presupposition of all such understanding of others is a knowledge of our own mental processes. The nearness to one's own personality is therefore undoubtedly one of the obstacles to an objective description of the functions of the ego.

This difficulty can easily be observed in clinical experience. Patients often admit without great resistance objectionable tendencies which the psychoanalyst shows them are in their unconscious and outside their actual ego. Just because these condemned and repressed tendencies are outside the actual personality, they can be admitted, and the patient can comfort himself by saying: "These strange things are in my unconscious, but not in me, i.e., not in the part of my personality which I feel to be my ego." The real conflict arises only after the unconscious tendencies begin to enter the ego and the patient begins to feel them as part of his actual personality.

Another reason that it seems paradoxical for our knowledge of the ego to be less advanced than that of the unconscious parts of the personality is that the ego is far more complicated and advanced in development than the id, which is a reservoir of the primary forces, or than the super-ego, which is a kind of complex of highly differentiated conditioned reflexes and reflex inhibitions.

What can be said with certainty about the ego is that it is a formation of two perceptive surfaces, one directed toward the instinctual life (inner perception), the second directed toward external reality (sense perception). One main function of the ego is to confront the facts of inner perception with the results of sense perception, *i.e.*, to bring subjective demands in harmony with the external circumstances. Its tendency is to find satisfaction for as many of the subjective needs and wishes as possible under existing external circumstances. The conscious ego is the most plastic part of the mental apparatus since it can adjust the behavior at any moment to a given situation, in contrast to reflex and automatic behavior which is fixed and predetermined in a much higher degree. Automatic reactions are rigid and adjusted to certain stimuli and so cannot adjust themselves to a sudden change in the external situation, whereas the ego has the capacity of performing adjustments *ad hoc.*

The functioning of the whole mental apparatus can be described approximately as follows: Instinctual needs and tendencies arising in the id tend to become conscious, because the conscious ego controls the motor innervations on which the satisfaction of the needs is dependent. A great part of the instinctual demands becomes immediately conscious and finds its acceptance or rejection after a process of conscious deliberation. This deliberation involves an estimate of the external situation and a comparison of the inner demand in question with other conflicting tendencies present in consciousness. For example, if someone had to decide whether he really wanted to attend a lecture or go to a theatre, there would be a conscious conflict which could be solved by a conscious judgment. Such tendencies and conflicts, however, have nothing whatever to do with repression. In such a case one desire is abandoned because it is incompatible with another more important. Repression, however, is a function which excludes certain tendencies from becoming conscious. It only occurs in cases in which the mere existence of a wish, irrespective of its realization, would cause an unbearable conscious conflict. To mention only one typical example, hostile feelings against a benefactor would tend to be repressed because they destroy our good opinion of ourselves. Similar non-social tendencies, to which the susceptibility of different individuals varies on account of the differences in their infantile experience, are inhibited even before they can become con-

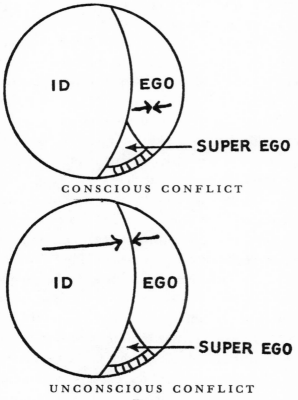

CONSCIOUS CONFLICT

UNCONSCIOUS CONFLICT

FIG. 3

scious. Repression, in contrast to conscious rejection, is a process of inhibition which arises on a deeper level of personality—somewhere on the borderline between id and ego—and saves the conscious personality from becoming aware of a painful conflict.

It is obvious that such an unconscious inhibiting process presupposes a kind of unconscious inner perception which leads to automatic, almost reflex inhibitions, similar to a conditioned reflex. This unconscious censoring function we ascribe to the super-ego. Repression is consequently based on a kind of unconscious censorship which reacts automatically to unacceptable tendencies. Although this process appears to us as a kind of unconscious selective judgment, which excludes certain definite tendencies from consciousness, nevertheless we have to assume that it operates schematically, is incapable of subtle differentiation and reacts uniformly to certain emotional factors in spite of their actual and sometimes important differences. It is comparable with a conditioned reflex rather than with a deliberate judgment. To cite a trivial example—the repression of the first incestuously tinged sexual strivings of the child establishes a general pattern of sexual repression which persists in later life, so that at the reawakening of sexuality in adolescence there is a general timidity and inhibition. The sexual impulse, although it has now lost its manifestly incestuous character and is directed to acceptable exogamous objects, suffers from the intimidations of the childhood. The super-ego lacks the capacity for making finer distinctions and represses sexuality in general without being able to recognize that the object of striving is no longer the same as in childhood. The well-known picture of the adolescent as shy and inhibited shows the result of this automatic process of restriction. In short, repression is always exaggerated and involves tendencies which the conscious ego would not reject if they became conscious. This important automatic and over-severe inhibiting function of the super-ego appears as one of the most general causes of psychoneurotic disturbances. Psychoneurotic symptoms are the dynamic results of unbearable tensions occasioned by the weight of exaggerated repressions.

Let us now describe the act of repression more fully. It starts with the super-ego's inner perception of a dynamic tension which tends to become conscious in order to induce the motor innervations necessary for its release. If the tendency is in conflict with the code of the super-ego, the conscious ego rejects it from fear, which is the motive power of repression. The ego, acting on the cue given by the super-ego, rejects the condemned id-tendency and so produces what we call repression. The fear felt by the ego for the super-ego is the signal which warns the ego to repress, and this intimidation of the ego by the super-ego can be considered as the continuation of the pressure which the parents brought to bear upon the child during the period of education.

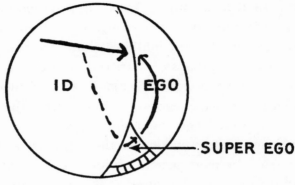

FIG. 4

The dotted line represents the inner perception of the repressed tendency by the super-ego. Repression is like a reflex arc consisting of a sensory and a motor part. The dotted line represents the sensory part, the arrow starting in the section, super-ego, and continued in the ego, the motor part. Repression is an automatic or reflectory inhibition.

The ego is exposed to two directing forces: the individual needs arising from the id on the one hand, and their denial by the super-ego on the other. Its tendency is to compromise between the two forces by modifying the id-tendencies in a way which is compatible with the code of the super-ego. This process we call domestication or sublimation of the original, inherited, non-social demands. Sublimation is what occurs in normal adjustment. The neurotic and psychotic personality is characterized by a relatively small capacity for sublimation.[1] These pathological personalities stubbornly hold on to their original tendencies, which they cannot carry out, because, paradoxically enough, they have at the same time developed a harsh super-ego. They are both over-social and non-social at the same time.

The Theory of Symptom-Formation

In neurotic personalities, owing to the lack of sufficient sublimation or of direct gratification, the only way for the ego to find relief from the pressure of unadjusted and repressed tendencies is to offset in some way the super-ego's rejection of them. There are two common mechanisms by which relief, in the form of neurotic and psychotic symptoms, is found. The first was early described by Freud as the method of distortion. The non-social tendencies cannot appear themselves in consciousness, but they send into consciousness substitute expressions by means of different complicated processes such as allusions, analogies and symbols. In this concealed manner they can appear in consciousness but they lose connection with the rest

[1] The *absolute* rate of the capacity for sublimation may in certain cases of neuroses be great, but then the inhibition of unsublimated gratifications makes the need for sublimations greater than the neurotic is able to perform—hence the production of symptoms.

of mental life. They are unintelligible, isolated, foreign bodies in the personality, disconnected from the rest of the conscious mental processes.

Since we had recognized the super-ego's faculty of an immediate inner perception of unconscious tendencies their distortion cannot be considered as an effective means to avoid the super-ego's rejection. A guilty conscience, indeed, may arise without any conscious reasons. The distortion of unconscious tendencies serves merely the purpose of avoiding the violation of the conscious ego, but does not eliminate the super-ego's condemnation, which manifests itself in seemingly unmotivated fear and sense of guilt.

Only a few years ago I succeeded in showing that the most general mechanism, through which repressed tendencies appear in consciousness without violating the super-ego and consequently without creating conflict and fear, is a peculiar way of bribing the super-ego. The ego accedes to the educational principles represented by the super-ego by self-punishing mechanisms, offering suffering as a price for the gratification of non-social tendencies.

A primitive theory of criminal justice displays itself in this mechanism latent in the depths of the personality. The basis of this peculiar psychological method by which the ego severs its dependence from its super-ego is the view that punishment or suffering in general is able to expiate crime. This attitude, which still prevails in contemporary jurisprudence, considers punishment and crime currencies which can be exchanged at a certain rate. In the neurotic personality this principle is realized in the paradoxical need for punishment or suffering. The ego exploits the suffering attendant on neurotic symptoms as a kind of moral justification, or license to indulge forbidden wishes. The ego, caught between the pressure of the id-tendencies and the inhibitions of the super-ego, solves the conflict by complying with the super-ego in the form of suffering. It thus disarms the inhibiting super-ego, and now free from moral restriction is able to indulge id-tendencies in the form of neurotic symptoms. Every psychoneurosis is, therefore, a compromise between repressing and repressed forces in which suffering represents the compliance of the ego with the social claims of the super-ego, while gratification represents the acceptance of the non-adjusted tendencies of the id. As to further details regarding both of these mechanisms, the method of distortion and the bribing of the super-ego by suffering, I must refer to the literature, since it lies beyond the scope of this book to present the detailed observations which substantiate this theory.[1]

[1] F. Alexander: "The Psychoanalysis of the Total Personality." *Monograph Series of Nervous and Mental Diseases*, Vol. 52, 1930.

It should now be clear that neurotic and psychotic symptoms are the result of a schematic and automatic process of repression which creates an extreme tension of the original tendencies which have been denied realization. Repression, however, is a function which originates in childhood. It is a product of education and has all the characteristics of a drill. Repression is the infantile way of controlling the original tendencies, since the infantile ego has not yet the ability either of judgment or of spontaneous renunciation. The only way to avoid the intolerable feeling of thwarting is the drastic exclusion from consciousness of tendencies which cannot be realized. After these inhibitions have once become automatically established in childhood, they have the tendency of all automatisms to persist. There are many reasons for assuming that the neurotic ego makes a more extensive use of repression to control the instinctual life than the normal one.

The ego of the adult psychoneurotic, which is usually well developed, could easily digest and modify the original tendencies and could also renounce some of them if it only knew about them. Through repression, however, the ego is separated from the instinctual life, and this situation is reflected in the diminished

T. Reik: *Geständniszwang und Strafbedürfnis.* Internationale Psychoanalytische Bibliothek, Nr. XVIII, 1935.

amount of freely dispensable mental energy in the neurotic personality. Repression is a more comfortable way of controlling unadjusted tendencies than conscious rejection, denial or modification, but it is too radical a method. The price which the neurotic pays for this comfort is his mental health and it is too high. He spares himself the painful struggle between temptation and its denial but, in doing so, he sacrifices most of his freely dispensable mental energy.

The Theoretical Foundation of the Psychoanalytic Technique

The technique of psychoanalytic therapy follows consistently from these concepts. The aim of therapy can be formulated as an attempt to replace the automatic restrictions of the super-ego by conscious judgment. Wide therapeutic experience has shown that with psychoneurotics this can be undertaken without danger, for their egos are capable of controlling the instinctual life if they come in contact with it. Naturally the removal of repression burdens the conscious personality with painful insight and a new problem, creating a conscious conflict. It also increases the responsibility of the conscious personality by extending its field of activity over hitherto unconscious portions of mental life. But this is the only way of changing those dynamic conditions in the personality which furnish the basis of psychoneuroses.

As long as tendencies remain unconscious they cannot undergo modification and sublimation because sublimation is precisely the result of the interplay of individual tendencies with the environment and constitutes adjustment to external reality. The conscious ego is the portion of the personality which is in touch with the environment; therefore, all psychological content, all instinctual demands and wishes, which are excluded from consciousness, remain isolated from environmental influences and retain their original unadjusted infantile qualities; they cannot undergo those transformations which we call reality adjustment. Therefore, repression makes the adjustment of instincts impossible. Only after it has been brought to consciousness can the ego modify and sublimate the mental energy bound up in the psychoneurotic symptoms.

In psychoanalytic technique there are two efficient factors at work replacing infantile super-ego-reactions by conscious judgment. One is intellectual, the other highly emotional. The first is the method of free association. By this method conscious control of trains of association is eliminated, and if the process is continued over a sufficient length of time, material of which the patient was previously unaware is gradually brought to the surface. In the exclusion from consciousness of certain tendencies there is, in addition to unconscious repression, a conscious and voluntary selective process called "suppression," which eliminates from the focus of interest everything which is even loosely connected with unconscious material. Suppression also eliminates all kinds of irrelevant material which would distract the attention from the topic which is at the focus of interest at any given moment. The elimination of the conscious control in trains of thought is a technique which is easy to acquire and is, in fact, nothing but overcoming suppression. If this is done, the tendency of unconscious material to express itself has to contend only with repression, the unconscious dynamic factor, and unconscious material begins to pour into consciousness. One might cite the analogy of a spring compressed by two weights. If one weight is removed, the spring will expand.

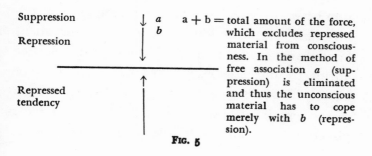

Suppression

Repression

Repressed
tendency

$a + b =$ total amount of the force, which excludes repressed material from consciousness. In the method of free association a (suppression) is eliminated and thus the unconscious material has to cope merely with b (repression).

Fig. 5

At the same time the emotional factor begins to appear, for the patient soon notices that the unconscious material which he so harshly condemns is not condemned or even evaluated by the psychoanalyst. He sees that the psychoanalyst is interested only in understanding the origin and meaning of these manifestations and does not pass any judgment upon them. With this assurance, the unconscious becomes gradually bolder and bolder, and exhibits itself with increasing frankness and clarity. What really happens is that the patient's ego loses more and more of its dependence on the super-ego and he transfers his emotional dependence to the psychoanalyst in adopting the same emotional attitude toward him that he previously had toward his super-ego. Since the super-ego is a precipitate of early education, an inwardly embodied image of the parents, the transference of the rôle of the patient's super-ego to the analyst results in a reproduction of the child-parent relationship during the analytic sessions. The analysis of the relation between patient and analyst corroborates unambiguously this theoretical description, and the patient himself very soon detects that his emotional behavior during treatment is often a strikingly exact copy of his childhood behavior. This revival during analysis of the emotional reactions of childhood, that have played so important a rôle in causing the psychoneurosis, offers a unique opportunity of understanding and reconstructing the pathogenic situations of the patient's past. The repetition of past emotional experiences in the relationship between patient and psychoanalyst Freud called "transference," and the renewal of the infantile conflict in the transference he described as the development of a "transference-neurosis" which goes hand in hand with the disappearance of the actual neurotic symptoms. The same tendency which created the symptom now expresses itself directly in the patient's emotional reactions to the psychoanalyst.

At this point it is important to emphasize that this kind of emotional relationship between patient and physician develops spontaneously in any form of psychotherapy, even in the relation of a patient to the physician who treats his organic diseases. It is a commonplace that in the presence of a physician who has succeeded in gaining the confidence of the patient, the subjective mental state of the patient is relieved, and that very often his symptoms, in so far as they are psychologically determined, improve. The most important therapeutic contribution of psychoanalysis consists in the psychological understanding and conscious handling of the transference. There was a time at the beginning of psychoanalysis when Freud was not yet able to estimate correctly the significance of this period when the symptoms disappear as a result of the transference-neurosis. Analyses interrupted at this stage, however, afforded only temporary relief and it soon became apparent that overcoming the transference-neurosis was a necessary part of therapy, for it effected only a pseudo-cure by changing the outlet of neurotic tendencies without permanently altering the relation of the ego to the instinctual life.[1]

The elimination of the transference-neurosis takes place only in what we refer to roughly as the second part of the analytic treatment. The advantage of the transformation of neurotic symptoms into transference manifestations lies in the fact that the transference manifestations are transparent, can be easily verbalized and so made conscious. The experienced psychoanalyst becomes able not only to understand the meaning of the transference manifestations but also to help the patient in finding precisely those verbal expressions which describe his emotional attitude. By these interpretations, the analyst forces the patient's ego to understand and face those psychic tendencies which were previously repressed. To sum up briefly: In the relaxed and matter-of-fact atmosphere of the psychoanalytic sessions the patient is en-

[1] One of the earliest analytic treatments which was interrupted during the phase of the "transference-neurosis" is Freud's famous case "Dora," which—a partial failure—gave Freud the first opportunity to realize the importance of the "transference."

couraged to express himself in intelligible language instead of in the distorted language of his symptoms. The next step is to force the conscious ego to recognize the meaning of these transparent manifestations.

An important quantitative factor still remains to be discussed. It is important to realize how much better capable the adult patient's conscious personality is to face and assimilate repressed tendencies than his infantile ego was at the time when they were originally repressed. In psychoanalytical treatment a fully developed adult ego is called upon to face tendencies which the infantile ego could not endure. On the other hand, the transference manifestations, though qualitatively the same as the corresponding emotions of childhood, are quantitatively much less intense. Transference can be considered as a kind of "shadow play" of childhood. When the patient, for example, exhibits toward the psychoanalyst the same hostility which was originally directed toward the father, this emotion is not likely to have the same intensity it had in youth, because the actual situation to which this emotion belonged no longer exists. The transference emotion is merely a projection of the past into the analytic situation and the analytic situation is in reality nothing more than the relation between patient and physician. These transference manifestations occur under the continuous control of the ego and the patient is constantly aware of their objectively unmotivated nature. The essential point is that, in the transference, the adult with his stronger and more resistant ego faces in reduced quantity the same kind of conflict which as a child his weak ego could not solve. The solution of the reduced emotional conflict effects an increase in the conscious ego's capacity for resistance, so that the ego becomes able to face mental conflicts and situations which were previously unbearable. This principle of analytic treatment can be compared with that of active immunization, by means of which the resistance of the body is partially increased by fighting small quantities of toxin.

The best experimental test of the correctness of this description is the fact that as a result of the correct interpretation of the transference situation, the corresponding forgotten infantile memories as a rule reappear in consciousness. The ego no longer has any reason for excluding the memory of past situations, which it has forgotten only because of associations with unbearable emotions.

The essence of psychoanalytic treatment consists— as we see—of three fundamental processes: (1) expression (abreaction) of repressed emotions (2) intellectual insight into the nature of formerly repressed material (3) remembering of repressed infantile memories. All these three therapeutic factors are closely interrelated and dependent upon one another. For example, the occurrence of infantile memories is often, though not always, connected with emotional abreaction; intellectual insight on the other hand may prepare the way for emotional abreaction and recollections; and emotional experience, if not overwhelmingly intense, is the only source of real insight. Without recollection and emotional abreaction, intellectual insight remains theoretical and ineffective. Neither is the mere expression of the unconscious tendencies, which sustained the symptom, in itself sufficient to secure a lasting cure. The patient must assimilate the formerly repressed psychic energies by bringing them in harmony with the rest of his personality. This is the meaning of what we call understanding or insight and this is what makes the free disposal of the formerly symptom-bound energy possible.

This harmonizing or integrating function of the ego is generally considered a faculty on which the analyst has to rely like the surgeon on the regenerative faculties of the tissues, but to which he cannot contribute much by his therapeutic activity. Yet, every correct interpretation helps the patient to connect the new material emerging from his unconscious with the rest of his conscious mind, with his past and present experience.

The psychoanalytic cure consists of the combination of these two processes: (1) the inviting of unconscious material into consciousness, and (2) the assimilation of this material by the conscious ego. To the first phase our literature refers by different expressions: emotional experience, abreaction, transformation of unconscious into conscious material; the second phase is called insight, digestion or assimilation of unconscious material by the ego or synthesis and integration.

Seen in this perspective psychoanalytic treatment appears not only as an analytic but also as a synthetic process.

The fact that we are able to describe in this way the psychological processes which take place during the treatment gives the psychoanalytic treatment a unique position in the field of psychiatry. In psychoanalysis we are able to follow the psychological processes in the patient during treatment and that makes analysis a reasoned and exact psychological method in contrast to all other current psychotherapeutic measures which, whether successful or not, are based much more on vague empirical observations than on a thorough understanding of the therapeutic process itself. Knowledge of the therapeutic mechanism is, however, the only way of gradually improving therapeutic technique. Although the efficiency of quinine was known before the biological basis of malaria was understood, a therapeutic measure can be considered scientific only when its use is based on a detailed knowledge of underlying processes, rather than on a fortuitous discovery of its effects.

It should now be clear that the application of psychoanalytic technique is limited to cases which fulfill certain conditions. The therapeutic theory is that the conscious ego, having been burdened by the knowledge of repressed tendencies, will be able to control them and dispose of them without conflict in an acceptable manner. This expectation implies the assumption that the adult patient's ego no longer needs the automatic regulation acquired in childhood and represented by the categorical rule of the super-ego, because the ego itself has acquired during the process of mental growth normative principles which guarantee adjusted behavior. Many years of experience have proved that in the great majority of psychoneuroses these conditions are fulfilled. There is no danger of turning the psychoneurotic into a species of criminal by removing his repressions. On the contrary, the psychoneurotic, relieved of his repressions, becomes better adjusted socially, because he has found a satisfactory compromise between his subjective needs and the demands of society. It was precisely the over-emphasis on repression which created an unbearable tension within him and prevented the originally non-social tendencies from undergoing modification, domestication, and sublimation. The original non-social tendencies, when repressed, preserve their non-social form and have to find artificial outlet in neurotic symptoms. The penetration of these tendencies into consciousness takes place only gradually and in small quantities during the treatment, and the ego therefore has time gradually to acquire control of these explosive forces and to apply them to normal social activities.

There are, however, unquestionably cases in which the fitness and maturity of the conscious ego cannot be counted on. I am thinking chiefly of two groups of personalities: (1) certain infantile types in which the ego is not fully developed, and which, consequently, cannot stand the process of analysis which burdens the weak ego with new conscious responsibilities and (2) certain types of schizophrenics. The schizophrenic ego betrays its weakness in the fact that under the pressure of subjective needs it is willing to give up its basic function, testing reality, and to sacrifice sense perception for hallucinations and delusions, falsifying reality in accordance with its subjective needs. In both these cases, infantiles and certain types of schizophrenics, the employment of the psychoanalytic technique, as I have described it, is not practicable without a preliminary treatment, the aim of which is to strengthen and reëducate the ego. The demand for this, however, is as yet hardly more than theoretical, as we are not yet able to determine the psychological influences by which an ego which has failed to develop normally may be strengthened. We are also still ignorant of the extent to which defects in the ego are due to inherited constitutional factors.

Psychoanalysis does not claim to be able to cure all forms of mental disturbance or all kinds of pathological personalities. It only maintains that all future methods of psychotherapy must be based on an understanding of the fundamental psychodynamic processes just as organic medicine has founded its therapeutic measures on an understanding of the underlying physicochemical processes. An insight into fundamental psychodynamic structure is the principal contribution of psychoanalysis to psychiatry.

III.

Critical Considerations on the Psychoanalytic Treatment of Psychoses

THE psychodynamic approach to the understanding of mental disturbances can be considered as a decisive step for the whole of psychopathology. It is due to this new point of view that psychopathology has overcome its merely descriptive stage and has become an explanatory science. The psychodynamic approach has also made it possible to influence psychopathological processes in an intelligent and systematic way, even if an extensive application of the analytical technique has been hitherto restricted to milder disturbances such as psychoneuroses.

As was pointed out in the second chapter, the psychoanalytic treatment of the psychoneuroses is based upon the fact that the psychoneurotic ego is able to face and make an acceptable use of those tendencies which were repressed by the weak, under-developed ego in childhood. This fact can be formulated by saying that the ego of the psychoneurotic is relatively well-developed and that the disturbance of the personality is based upon an early break between the ego and the emotional and instinctual life. The therapeutic problem consists merely in a rebuilding of this disturbed connection between the instinctual life and the ego. As has already been briefly explained, the employment of the psychoanalytic technique as used with psychoneurotics is strictly dependent upon a relatively well-developed ego. In all cases of psychic disturbances in which this condition is not fulfilled, the application of the psychoanalytic technique without important modifications seems in advance to be out of place. In all cases in which we have to assume that the ego itself is under-developed and lacking those faculties which differentiate the adult ego from the childhood ego, the capacity to estimate, to accept and reject, to endure tensions and deprivations, the psychoanalytic technique cannot be used with advantage because it forces the ego to cope with a problem which it is unable to accomplish. The effective means employed by the infantile ego to protect itself from emotional situations which it cannot master is repression. To force an ego to use other measures of which it is genuinely incapable would be a senseless procedure.

It seems that, at least in a large number of cases, the

schizophrenic suffers from a constitutionally or developmentally conditioned weakness of the ego. Nevertheless, in recent years, attempts to cure severe cases of psychosis by analytic means have become more frequent, although the therapeutic value of these experiments has been much debated. It is worth while to stop for a moment to review critically the work done and the methods employed. Such a critical review has proved necessary and fruitful in every science, for the investigator, submerged in daily routine, easily loses his judgment and is inclined to fall into a rut, uncritically employing highly developed and specialized methods in the treatment of cases which are different. There is an imminent danger, since psychoanalysis has begun to experiment with psychoses, that this highly specialized method may be employed in the treatment of cases to which it is not strictly applicable.

As is well known, the psychoanalytic method of investigation and therapy was originally limited to certain types of psychoneuroses. But the rich harvest of psychological knowledge of general application has induced psychoanalysts to study new types of cases from the same point of view and to test the efficiency of analytic therapy on other mental disturbances than those for which the technique was originally designed. It seems to me of great importance to distinguish in the extension of psychoanalytic methods between research and therapy. The employment of psychoanalytic knowledge for the understanding of other mental disturbances than the psychoneuroses which were first investigated is legitimate, but the same therapeutic procedure with other kinds of cases is highly problematic. It is certain that illnesses with a different psychodynamic structure require modifications in the technique.

As a matter of fact, a modification of technique proved necessary when psychoanalysis was first applied to children. In child-analysis the technique used with adults was found inadequate because the same coöperation cannot be expected from a child as from an adult, and the child cannot be induced to assume the mental attitude required by the method of free association. In the place of free association, Melanie Klein introduced the ingenious method of the play-technique.[1] She observed the playing child and interpreted the products of its phantasy displayed during spontaneous play. By means of this change in technique, however, she tried to make the child conscious of the latent meaning of the manifestations of its unconscious, so that Melanie Klein's technique, although better adjusted to the nature of the child, is

---

[1] Melanie Klein: "Infant Analysis," *Int. Journal of Psychoanalysis,* Vol. 7.

based essentially upon the original therapeutic principle of making repressed material conscious.

Anna Freud in her technique of child analysis [1] went even further in changing the original principles. She took into consideration the fact that in children the dynamic relation between the impulses and the ego is different than in adults. The child's ego is relatively weak but at the same time flexible. Anna Freud, therefore, tried to influence it directly in an educational sense on the one hand, and on the other she tried to estimate more carefully the extent to which the child's weak ego can be burdened with interpretations, *i.e.*, the knowledge of repressed material.

I mention the technique of child-analysis only as an example of the necessity of changing the technique in applying it to new and different therapeutic fields. It is only natural that there is a demand to make use of experiences obtained from the study of psychoneurotics in the treatment of psychoses. In the following pages I shall restrict myself to the problem of applying analysis to schizophrenic psychoses. According to Abraham's and other psychoanalysts' experience with manic-depressives, it seems that the original psychoanalytic technique does not require essential

[1] Anna Freud: "Introduction to the Technique of Child Analysis," *Nervous and Mental Diseases, Monograph Series,* Vol. 48.

modification in these cases, although apparently not all disturbances of this category are susceptible of psychoanalytic treatment.[1]

If one considers the problem of treating schizophrenic psychoses from a superficial and merely technical point of view, the only concrete difficulty in applying analytic technique appears to lie in the difficulty of securing the coöperation of the psychotic patient in establishing rapport with the physician. In many cases this difficulty is only temporary and prevails only during severe psychotic episodes, so that analytical technique could be tried in the lucid intervals, when the patient often displays not only a considerable capacity for "transference," but even a great desire for emotional contact with others. In such cases the external conditions for the employment of analytic technique are fulfilled.

The most direct and simple way of deciding whether the treatment applicable to neurosis is also feasible in cases of psychosis would undoubtedly be experiment, but in medicine experimentation is to a certain extent limited by a therapeutic interest in the welfare of the patient. Senseless and presumably unsuccessful or even harmful experiments must be excluded. Unfortunately, our knowledge of the

[1] It seems that the importance of psychogenic factors is not the same in all cases of manic-depressive disturbances.

specific structure of neurotic and psychotic personalities is not yet far enough advanced to enable us to
decide definitely from purely theoretical considerations whether the analytic method is applicable to
psychoses without essential modification.

Actual experience is still insufficient to permit a
decisive opinion. Up to the present, psychoanalytic
treatments have generally been applied in an ambula-
tory way, which with psychoses is generally difficult
and risky. Partly for this practical reason, and partly
also from theoretical considerations, the general attitude among psychoanalysts has been that the diagnosis
of schizophrenia is a contra-indication for psychoanalytic treatment. In recent years, however, there has
been a change in this rigid attitude and in some of
the psychiatric hospitals psychoanalysis has become an
accepted method, as for example in Bloomingdale
Hospital, the Shepherd and Enoch Pratt Hospital and
in the McLean Hospital in America. E. Simmel in
Berlin, and B. Glueck and the Menninger brothers
in America have opened psychoanalytic sanitariums
for analytic treatment of hospitalized patients, and
although detailed and critical reports are still lacking,
all these institutions have encouraged a more opti-
mistic attitude.

In contrast to this, however, is the fact which experienced analysts have repeatedly observed, that

psychoanalytic treatment may precipitate schizophrenic episodes in cases where latent schizophrenia had not been diagnosed before the analysis.[1] I, myself, have had occasion to observe cases in which I could not explain the onset of an episode otherwise than as a reaction to the analytic approach. Experiences of this sort have made me cautious, and without formulating definite theoretical principles for all cases in which schizophrenia was suspected and in which nevertheless I undertook a psychoanalytic treatment, I changed my technique. With a changed technique, I could see positive results, or at least avoid reactive episodes, and most psychoanalysts who have reported on the treatment of psychoses have agreed that they have also found it necessary to change their technique. A. A. Brill reported several cases in which he had good results with a modified technique,[2] and G. Zilboorg emphasizes the necessity of a "long preliminary period of reality testing," in which the analyst

[1] L. E. Hinsie remarks that there are only "impressionistic comments" in the literature, that psychoanalysis has a detrimental influence on the management of schizophrenic patients. The precipitating influence of the "classical technique" in cases of latent schizophrenia is, however, a well-established experience. L. E. Hinsie: *The Treatment of Schizophrenia*, p. 169. The Williams and Wilkins Co., Baltimore, 1930.

[2] It would be highly desirable if a psychoanalyst of A. A. Brill's experience gave further details as to the modifications that he mentions in his article, "Schizophrenia and Psychotherapy," *American Journal of Psychiatry*, Vol. IX.

should gain the positive transference of the patient.[1]
L. E. Hinsie's thorough study, *The Treatment of
Schizophrenia,* in which he gives an extensive review
of the various modifications in technique suggested by
psychiatrists and psychoanalysts, also deserve mention.

The fact of psychotic reactions to the analytic approach is, paradoxically enough, by no means an
unfavorable sign, for it shows that the course of a
psychosis can be influenced by psychological influences and it is a question of secondary importance
whether this influence has hitherto been exercised in
a favorable or unfavorable direction. Once the essential fact is established that the course of a psychosis
yields to psychological treatment, there is a theoretical
possibility that an intelligent method may be invented
by which cures could be effected.

It is impossible to form a definite opinion on the
possibilities of the psychoanalytic treatment of psychoses as long as there are no reports which give an
exact description of the technique employed instead
of simply reporting positive or negative results. The
psychoanalytic treatment of psychoneuroses is sufficiently developed and refined for us to give a de-

[1] The same remark applies also to G. Zilboorg's article, "Affective
Reintegration in the Schizophrenias," *Archives of Neurology and
Psychiatry,* Vol. 24. The expression which he uses: "a long preliminary period of reality testing," implies a modification of technique,
by means of which the usually loose relation of the schizophrenic
ego to reality is reconstructed.

tailed account of its different therapeutic factors. We
can follow the process of the cure and know with fair
precision what is going on in the mind of the patient.
Psychoanalytic treatment today is no longer based on
rough observation but on a detailed knowledge of the
mental apparatus and of the dynamic structure of the
psychoneuroses. A blind application of psychoanalytic
technique would be contrary to its scientific nature,
and as we know the basic differences between the
dynamic structure of psychoses and neuroses, we
should be able at least to outline those modifications
in technique which follow necessarily from the
differences between the psychotic and the neurotic
minds. I shall restrict myself to a few fundamental
considerations which should be regarded merely as
suggestions to be tested in the future by clinical experience.

We may define the chief difference between psychoses and psychoneuroses by stating that whereas the
psychoneurosis is chiefly a conflict between the different structual parts of the mental apparatus, in
psychosis the relation of the mental apparatus to the
external world is profoundly disturbed. The psychotic, during episodes or in progressive stages, continually loses his orientation in the external world
because he falsifies the data of his sense-perceptions.
To express it simply, the psychotic is so largely sub-

ject to the pressure of his subjective non-adjusted
demands that he cannot accept a reality which opposes
them and falsifies the picture of the external world
which his senses and normal thinking offer him, and
so sees things other than they really are. The most
extreme forms of this falsification of reality are hallucinations, but illusions and even delusions have a
similar significance. This falsifying tendency has a
transparent mechanism in delusions in which the
psychotic perceives in himself unacceptable hostile
or sexual tendencies and simply refuses to accept
them as his own mental possessions and projects them
on others. The well-known resistance of paranoiacs
against all explanations of their symptoms, and the
impossibility of convincing them of the error of their
delusions, is based upon the fact that they actually
perceive hostile or sexual emotions in themselves.
Their error consists only in wrongly locating these
emotions. Feeling the presence of their emotions, they
will not admit that they belong to their own personality and so incorrigible delusions arise, the vividness
of which is based on the actual inner experience of
the projected emotions. We may express this otherwise by saying that the psychotic has, in a sense, no
respect for reality. It is easier for him to relinquish
his contact with reality than to control his own emotions, and as a result he solves his inner conflicts by

changing the picture of reality in accordance with the subjective demands.

At this point it is important to distinguish between two kinds of conflicts in psychotics. The first is of an infantile type and can be expressed in the following way: "The world is not as I should like to have it. I do not want to live in such a world and therefore prefer to live in a phantastic world, and am, therefore, ready to sacrifice real satisfactions and content myself with hallucinations of my own choosing."

The second type of conflict produces delusions and all paranoid phenomena and is the same as we find in psychoneuroses. These conflicts are no longer based upon the fact that external reality is contradictory to the subjective tendencies, but on the fact that certain emotional tendencies are not acceptable to the socially adjusted part of the ego, the super-ego. In the neuroses hostile and sexual tendencies, unacceptable to the super-ego, are repressed and returned in a disguised form as neurotic symptoms and find in this way a substitutive satisfaction. In the psychotic mechanisms the tendencies which are rejected not by external reality, but by the super-ego, are not repressed but projected. They are not recognized as one's own, but are attributed to external reality. While the paranoid mechanisms are falsifications of both internal and external reality, hallucinations and illusions are only falsifications of external reality. The hallucinating patient only changes the picture of the external world, but the paranoid denies something in himself.

It should now be evident that these two categories of symptoms, the simple falsification of reality and the paranoid symptoms, may provide the basis for a classification of the various forms of schizophrenia. The paranoid mechanisms resemble the neuroses more closely, for the more highly organized portions of the mental apparatus are still functioning. They show the dynamic efficiency of the socially adjusted part of the ego, for paranoid patients are not able to get rid of the influence of their super-ego. The fact that they project certain emotional tendencies proves that they cannot accept them. Repression, the method of the neurotic patient, is, however, impossible for them. Their ego is unable to exclude from consciousness those tendencies which the neurotic is able to conceal or distort. The paranoid psychotic cannot repress tendencies foreign to the ego nor can he accept them, and his only solution is projection. He is aware of these tendencies, but being unable to repress them must deny them as part of his own ego. Hallucinations and illusions do not presuppose such an inner conflict between the super-ego and the tendencies hostile to the ego, for they are merely solutions of a conflict between the ego and external reality. This mechanism is, therefore, more infantile, because it corresponds to an early stage of development in which the conflict between subjective demands and reality is not yet inwardly reproduced as a conflict between subjective demands and the super-ego.

Paranoid hallucinations occupy an intermediary position, for in them the threats of the super-ego are projected on external reality in an attempt to get rid of the super-ego. If we remember that the super-ego has developed by assuming and embodying the moral and educational prescriptions of the parents, paranoid hallucinations may be considered as a regression to the period in which the ego was controlled merely by others, and the child sacrificed his desires from fear of his parents' restrictions.

In many cases of schizophrenia, the ego also loses its synthetic function of harmonizing the different and often contradictory instinctual demands. The sudden unmotivated aggressive attacks and self-destructive behavior are clear signs of disintegration in the structure of the ego. It seems to me unjustified to regard the impulsive self-mutilations of schizophrenics as the self-punishing reactions of a harsh super-ego. It is impossible to assume that the schizophrenic, who is no longer guided by the fundamental dictates of the super-ego, such as pity and disgust, and who indulges in coprophilia, should at the same time be affected by the exquisitely moral need for punish-ment. The self-mutilations, although symbolic of self-castrations, are rather manifestations of isolated passive-female wishes, which find an outlet after the synthetic function of the ego is eliminated. The poly-morphous, rhapsodic behavior is the manifestation of disorganized instinctual demands which have lost their interconnections and seek outlets independently of each other.

These considerations indicate a distinction between two main groups of schizophrenia, the one character-ized by the predominance of paranoid symptoms (paranoid hallucinations and delusions) , the other by simple falsifications, hallucinations and illusions. The theoretical and therapeutic evaluation of cases with pronounced paranoid symptoms must be different from those which do not exhibit them. The paranoid cases display a greater participation of the super-ego and show that the ego structure is less deteriorated than in the other class. A common factor in both cases, however, is the amazing ease with which the psychotic gives up his connection with reality and falsifies it according to his subjective demands. The general characteristic of schizophrenia is consequently the ability to dispense with reality which differenti-ates it fundamentally from neuroses in which such a radical flight from reality is impossible. The neurotic is too loyal to reality to be able to deny its objective nature and, consequently, must work out the conflict within himself. The dynamic relation between the ego and the instinctual demands is exactly the opposite in psychoses and neuroses. In neuroses the ego overpowers the instinctual demands—the neurotic symptom is a protest of the restricted instincts—but in psychoses the ego is weak in relation to the instinctual demands, hence the apparent lack or at least weakness of repression. In psychoses the instinctual demands overpower the ego, and the ego, following the pressure of these demands, abandons its oldest and first acquired function, the recognition of reality. At the same time, however, the ego loses its other function of harmonizing the different instinctual demands and turns out to be weak in the face of both external reality and the pressure of the primitive unadjusted instinctual tendencies.

Our knowledge of the developmental phases of the mind permits a more precise evaluation of the difference between psychoses and neuroses. We have many reasons for assuming that the infant's psychic processes are similar to those which adults manifest only in their dream life, and are also similar to hallucinations of schizophrenics. Many years ago, Bleuler referred to the similarity of dream processes and schizophrenic manifestations. The differentiation be-

tween an ego and a non-ego is undoubtedly one of
the first accomplishments in the individual's development, and the acceptance of or substitution by hallucinatory phantasies of the data of sense-perception is
the basis of this distinction. We may say, therefore, that
the hallucinating psychotic gives up his *first* adjustment to external reality, whereas in the neuroses
mainly, the *later,* social adjustment is disturbed.
The former is simply an adjustment of the
individual to the facts of physical reality and takes
place during the first two years after birth before the
differentiation between ego and super-ego has begun.
We must assume that patients who later develop
schizophrenia have not accomplished satisfactorily
this first step in development, and the distinction
between an ego and a non-ego had never been firmly
established in them.[1] Only a tenuousness in the relation to external reality can explain so radical a solution of mental conflicts.

The precipitating causes of psychoses, of course,
belong to adolescence or adult life, and we often observe precipitating conflicts of the same social nature
as are effective in neuroses. In his flight from the
conflicts of adult life, however, the psychotic reverts

[1] Storch very appropriately calls this phenomenon "*Grenzver-
wischung zwischen Ich und Umwelt.*" Dr. Alfred Storch: *Das
Archaisch-Primitive Erleben und Denken der Schizophrenen,* Julius
Springer, Berlin.

to a very early period when he was not yet able to distinguish between phantasy and reality, and it is precisely this depth of regression which is characteristic of psychoses. The developmental difference between psychoses and neuroses is that adjustment to reality in the former has been disturbed at a very early period, while in neuroses the disturbance dates from the emotional conflicts with others, parents and siblings, *viz.*, from the period of the development of the super-ego.

This early origin of schizophrenic symptoms allows us to make an etiological postulate that in schizophrenic psychoses the inherited constitution generally plays a more important rôle than in neuroses. It is difficult to imagine that external influences are alone responsible for this early weakness of the ego which interferes with the first adjustment to physical reality, unless we find in the majority of cases such unusual and violent psychological influences as can explain this early rejection of reality.

I admit that the etiological theory of the constitutional weakness of the "Ego-Anlage" is too general to be an altogether satisfactory scientific concept, but as ·long as we have nothing better to put in its place it may serve for general orientation and help us to avoid overemphasizing the psychogenic theory of schizophrenia. The influences of post-natal development may also play a very important rôle in many cases. All influences which strengthen the ego-reality relation, or all influences which tend to make external reality more acceptable even to a weak ego, will decrease the efficiency of psychotic tendencies; and *vice versa* all later influences which make it difficult for the ego to accept external reality will increase the likelihood of a schizophrenic attack. A specific etiological theory of schizophrenia, however, must explain why the conflicts and influences of later life can drive these personalities back to such an early stage of development when the mind was unable to distinguish between external and internal reality, between ego and non-ego. The weakness of the faculty for making this distinction cannot be explained by later influences, which occur after this distinguishing faculty has developed in normal course. Traumatic influences even of later infancy cannot be responsible for the weakness of a faculty, the acquirement of which belongs to an earlier phase of development. Many people do not like the world as it is, but only a few—and those are the psychotics—deny it so forcibly.

Although they do not formulate all these considerations so precisely, the therapeutic attempts of our modern psychiatric hospitals display an intuitive grasp of these facts. The general tendency in modern hospitals to make the environment as agreeable and acceptable as possible for the patients is a therapeutic measure quite in harmony with the views here developed. The positive results of occupational therapy can also be similarly explained. If the patient finds a place which he can fill successfully, he will be more inclined to reaccept at least a part of reality and abandon his flight from it. The principle of adjusting the institutional environment to the personality of schizophrenics is most consistently realized in the therapeutic methods of H. S. Sullivan.[1] He adjusts not only the physical but also the human environment to the emotional life of his patients by employing as attendants schizoid personalities who have lost their "natural conviction as to right and wrong," and who consequently have an understanding of the peculiarities of the insane. Furthermore, he specially trains these "sensitive, shy and ordinarily considered handicapped employees" by teaching them to "cease to regard the schizophrenics in more or less traditional ideology as insane," but instead to see the many points of significant resemblance between the patient and employee. Sullivan reports unusually good results.

The principle of selecting attendants with person-

---

[1] *Proceedings of the Second Colloquium on Personality Investigation*, pp. 46, 47, and 107. The Johns Hopkins Press, Baltimore.

ality traits similar in quality to the schizophrenic patients is in accordance with the observations of H. Nunberg [1] and K. Landauer,[2] that the reëstablishment of the patient's relation to the external world is based on an identification with the person or persons with whom he has continuous contact, and it is obvious that such an identification is more easily effected with individuals of a similar type. This also explains the frequency of pronounced homosexual tendencies in schizophrenics, for the homosexual object relation of schizophrenics is a pseudo-object relation, since it is essentially a narcissistic identification.

What we are now interested in, however, is to make use of this knowledge to find the general principles of an adequate and consistent psychotherapy for psychotics. It should now be clear that the classical psychoanalytic technique is by no means adapted to the specific conditions of the personality of psychotics. This method was invented in dealing with neurotics and is well adapted to the psychodynamic conditions of psychoneuroses. The problem of the neurotic personality is to regain possession of the repressed mental content which his adult ego might easily control if it only knew of it. The problem of the psychotic is quite

[1] H. Nunberg: "Der Verlauf des Libidokonfliktes in einem Falle von Schizophrenia." *Int. Zeitschrift fur Psychoanalyse,* Band VIII.
[2] Dr. K. Landauer, "Spontanheilung einer Katatonia," *Int. Zeitschrift fur ärztliche Psychoanalyse,* Bd. II.

different. The problem is not to release repressions, but to induce the ego to accept external reality. The neurotic must learn to accept repressed *psychological* facts, while the psychotic must learn to accept rejected *external* facts.

In a brief article on denial, Freud has shown that the infantile ego accepts everything from reality which agrees with the first libidinal demands and rejects everything opposed to them.[1] The first division between ego and non-ego takes place on this emotional basis. The ego is in the beginning a collection of everything that is good, acceptable and connected with pleasure, while everything that is bad and unacceptable belongs to the non-ego. Gradually from external reality more and more is accepted, but always more easily those things which we love. Probably the positive attitude toward the objects of the external world, object-love in distinction from narcissistic love, is that which is less developed in cases which later develop schizophrenia. The capacity to change narcissistic libido into object libido is less in the psychotic personality, and this seems to be a constitutional feature of the psychotic.

The aim of an intelligent psychotherapy should, therefore, be to increase the libidinal relations of the

---

[1] S. Freud: "Die Verneinung." *Gesammelte Schriften.* Bd. XI. Int. Psychoanalytischer Verlag, Vienna.

ego to the external world. How this principle is carried through in institutional treatment has already been described. In psychotherapeutic treatment the consistent fostering of a positive transference will remain the most important technical therapeutic device. In a noteworthy article, Nunberg described the cure of a catatonic episode,[1] and showed conclusively that during the treatment the physician as the object of a positive transference was the first point of crystallization in the gradually increasing acceptance of external reality. As a kind of catalyzer the analyst concentrates in himself all the positive feelings of which the patient is capable and during the healing process the patient directs this positive feeling from the psychoanalyst to other objects of reality. The psychotherapy of schizophrenia must be based on the systematic and deliberate handling of the positive transference, and also on the skillful steering of the further extension of positive feelings from the analyst to other objects. Especially this latter process is difficult, because schizophrenics after having accepted the analyst as the only object are apt to cling to him with an extremely strong passive-dependent attachment and refuse stubbornly to transfer their positive feelings from the analyst to other objects. All further details and technical devices must be based on practical ex-

[1] *Loc. cit.*

perimentation. Whether the interpretation and reconstruction of repressed mental content are justified in the treatment of psychoses is dependent upon the degree to which the psychosis is mixed with neurotic mechanisms. It seems to me quite evident, however, that the essentially psychotic process cannot be influenced by interpretation. The psychotic ego is weak in repression and so must deny and project, so that the therapeutic problem is not to resolve repressions but to strengthen the relation to external reality. I assume that paranoid types must be generally more accessible to psychotherapeutic methods and also that, in these cases, the classical technique of interpretation in the latter part of the treatment, after a strong positive transference has been established, may play an important rôle. This is because paranoid symptoms indicate the presence of neurotic mechanisms, which consist of conflicts between the wishes and the superego. I do not wish now to attempt to decide how much the original technique of interpretation can accomplish in such cases, after the analyst has succeeded in establishing a strong positive transference. This question can only be solved by systematic observation in psychiatric hospitals.

These theoretical considerations coincide with the few empirical observations which we possess, and which show that paranoid cases are as a matter of fact more easily influenced by psychological means than other forms of schizophrenia. Especially interesting in this respect is a case of paranoia, which Feigenbaum cured by using the psychoanalytic technique, because in this case Feigenbaum was able to define those psychological mechanisms which were primarily involved in the process of cure.[1] Also, we in the Chicago Psychoanalytic Institute in a severe case of paranoia, being treated at present by Helen McLean without any fundamental modifications of the psychoanalytic technique, can clearly follow step by step the rapidly progressing curative effect of the analytical procedure. These observations confirm our view according to which paranoias, especially those with well circumscribed and systematized delusions, constitute an intermediary group between neuroses and psychoses, and are more accessible to psychoanalytic treatment than other forms of schizophrenia. Yet, in the light of *all* these considerations we are also able to explain why the psychoanalytic approach, I mean especially interpretations, might sometimes precipitate an acute episode. Interpretations always imply a burdening of the ego and force the patient

---

[1] Dorian Feigenbaum: "Analysis of a Case of Paranoia Persecutoria: Structure and Cure," *The Psychoanalytic Review*, Vol. XVII, No. 2, April, 1930, and "Paranoia and Magic," *The Journal of Nervous and Mental Disease*, Vol. 72, No. 1, 1930. Feigenbaum notified me that this case, after nine years of observation, continued to remain well.

to see either an unwelcome part of external reality or of his own personality. The weak and non-resistant psychotic ego reacts naturally to the insight forced upon him, by flight, denial and falsification.

I have tried by these few suggestions merely to indicate the possibility of employing psychoanalytic knowledge in the development of a method really adapted to the specific psychodynamic conditions of schizophrenics. If I have demonstrated no more than that in psychoses the simple and uncritical use of a treatment designed for neuroses is inappropriate, I have fulfilled my purpose. In outlining the general principles of a future technique for the treatment of psychoses I have avoided calling it a psychoanalytic treatment and have used the more general expression, psychotherapy, in order to emphasize that what we usually call psychoanalytic treatment is especially adapted to the psychic condition of the neurotic. The new and modified technique, however, which I have tried to suggest here in very general outline, can only be based on psychoanalytic insight: Psychoanalysis is the name both for a method in therapy and for a theory of mental processes.

IV.

The Sociological and Biological Orientation of Psychoanalysis

ABOVE all, psychoanalysis can be characterized as a dynamic approach in as much as it considers mental life as the manifestation and intricate interplay of tendencies and strivings which ultimately express themselves in motor behavior. Apart from this dynamic feature, psychoanalysis has introduced into psychology two fundamental aspects, a sociological and a biological aspect.

The biological orientation consists in considering all the dynamic forces as biologically conditioned, as manifestations of those energy-consuming processes that constitute the biological phenomenon, "life." This biological aspect can be more easily discussed after the sociological implications of psychoanalysis have been described and we shall return to it later.

The sociological orientation can be briefly formulated as follows: The development of personality can be considered and understood, at least partially, as a process of adjustment of the original inherited phylo-genetically predetermined instinctive cravings to the requirements of collective life as they are represented by any given culture. This process of adjustment can be described as a process of domestication or socialization of the originally socially unadjusted individual. After birth a healthy individual can be considered as a biologically well-functioning organism which has, however, still to solve the problem of adjusting its biological needs to certain special conditions—namely, to the normative and restrictive requirements which every form of collective life organized in a cultural pattern represents.

The study of normal, psychoneurotic, and psychotic adults has shown that in no adult, not even in a normal one, does the whole personality participate in this process of domestication. No adult personality is a homogeneous entity. The socially adjusted conscious mental life, which contains the conscious motivations and connections between our actions, desires, hopes, and wishes, is only a surface phenomenon. A great part of our conscious psychological processes and overt behavior is at least partially determined by socially non-adjusted, non-conscious motivations.

The conscious portion of our personality, which

we feel as our conscious ego, which gives us the sense of continuity in our life, is a highly organized unit in which the various psychological tendencies, wishes, hopes, desires, and so forth, are related, subordinated, and coördinated with one another. This inner harmony of the ego system is based, however, on a dynamic phenomenon, on repression, by the help of which tendencies, motivations, any psychological content that is not adjusted to the social environment, is excluded from consciousness. Through repression the personality tries to exclude everything that would upset this harmony, all tendencies that would create a conflict with the dominating, socially adjusted tendencies and normative principles of the conscious personality.

Repression works according to principles that correspond to the general ideological principles of a given culture, and this eliminating and selective function of the personality is transmitted to the child through the process of education, through the influence of the family, especially through the parents who, as the representatives of the cultural milieu, are the mediators through whom this restrictive and normative influence on the personality takes place.

Repression is, therefore, a cultural phenomenon since the principles according to which repressions take place correspond to the moral code of a given civilization. The well-adjusted adult can be considered as a domesticated individual and a great portion of psychological abnormalities can be considered as the result of unsuccessful domestication, although as already emphasized, in no individual does the total personality take part in the process of domestication and everyone retains in his unconscious tendencies of an infantile nature that are not modified in a social sense. In neurotic and psychotic individuals we find a much higher proportion of such infantile tendencies, and neurotic and psychotic symptoms, as well as neurotic behavior in life, are expressions of these socially non-adjusted cravings. Viewed from a broad perspective, psychoneuroses and psychoses can be considered as a protest against the process of social adjustment. They represent the victory of the individualistic forces in defiance against the demands of collective life.

This dynamic concept has an important sociological implication, since it explains psychoneuroses and psychoses as a result of the clash of the inherited instinctive equipment of the individual with the demands of social life. Seen from this perspective, the so often quoted affinity between neurosis, psychosis, genius, and criminality is readily understandable. In the genius these individualistic tendencies take a creative form. The genius, like the psychopath or the criminal,

does not entirely conform to society; instead of con-
forming, he creates new socially acceptable expressions
of the instinctive forces. He impresses his formative
power upon civilization and changes it after his
own image. In criminality the individualistic tendency appears in a destructive form in the refusal to
accept a social code, but it fights the social code in a
destructive way and not like the genius by creating
new socially acceptable forms of expression.

Neurotic personalities may have both genius and
criminal in them, but they express both creative and
destructive tendencies only in phantasy in a symbolic
language which only they and not even their own
conscious personality can understand, a symbolic
language that is only the expression of their unconscious. Neurotic symptoms contain both creative and
destructive tendencies. They are, however, of no use
to anybody but the neurotic himself, for whom they
are an outlet for repressed tendencies which the
neurotic cannot carry through into reality, but which
he also cannot abandon or modify in a socially acceptable fashion. Through the symbolic medium of the
symptoms, they may give expression to the wish to
give birth to a child, but at the same time they express
destruction, murder, or cruelty by the same means of
symbolic representation.

In very rough outline, this is the sociological aspect

of psychoanalysis as a dynamic theory of personality development. It is socially oriented because it explains the problem which the individual has to solve during his development as the adjustment of the original inherited strivings to the social setting into which the individual happens to be born. The corner stone and the most dramatic phase of this process of social adjustment is known under the name of the Œdipus complex. It represents the conflict of the child with its first society, with the family, and the solution of the Œdipus complex is the most important step in social adjustment. It means the adjustment of the feelings of love and hate toward parents and siblings, which feelings are nurtured by the biologically conditioned cravings of sexuality and the destructive instincts.

This social orientation of psychoanalysis is by no means exhausted in the present state of our knowledge. The comparative study of neurotic and psychotic individuals in different cultures will allow a more precise identification of those regulative principles that are characteristic of different cultures. It will lead to a more precise description of those ideologies that have a formative influence upon personality development. Different cultures can be considered as different solutions of the problem of how individuals, with the same inventory of biologically predetermined instinctive forces, can adjust themselves to different forms of collective life. Such studies of the process of adjustment to different cultural patterns, and especially the study of the failures of adjustment, will contribute more to sociology, however, than to psychoanalysis proper. A better knowledge of the biological organism itself, a better understanding of the nature of those biologically conditioned forces that are exposed to the external cultural influences, must be expected from another direction, from the increasing biological orientation of psychoanalysis. This biological orientation, which characterizes the most recent developments of our field, brings it closer to its birthplace, to medicine, and contributes in a promising manner to the oldest problem the human mind has tried to solve since ancient times—the body-mind problem.

In the preceding discussion we have tried to describe the development of a personality after birth as an adjustment of the instinctive life to the conditions of collective life represented by the different cultural milieus. The specific economic and ideologic nature of a culture is the product of historical development which is independent of the particular individual who is born into this culture and who must then adjust himself to it. But the cultural pattern itself is not independent of the biological structure of those individuals who created these cultural patterns as a collective method of gratifying their biological needs. Every culture is itself conditioned not only historically, but in a more fundamental way, biologically. It is a formation of biological units living together in organized groups. The individual, however, is not born into such an organized group as a *tabula rasa,* as many sociologists erroneously believe. It is by no means an infinitely pliable object which later cultural influences can mold into anything, because its development, including personality development after birth, is in its principal features biologically predetermined. Man is by no means only a product of his environment, as often is postulated by social scientists. When he is born, he represents a complicated biological mechanism which is the product of a much older historical development than the culture to which he has to adjust himself after his birth. His body with its instinctive cravings is the product of the phylogenetic development which itself can be considered as a process of adjustment, an adjustment of the race to external physical conditions. The development of an individual in the womb from the moment of impregnation until birth is a brief recapitulation of the long history of this process of adjustment which his predecessors had to accomplish.

This embryological portion of the individual life

history appears as an automatic, merely mechanical process in comparison with the later personality development after birth, the adjustment to the social milieu which every individual has to solve for himself through active participation, through trial and error, through experience of pain and failure which force him to find those types of gratifications that are possible and acceptable in the society in which he is brought up. The development of the body seems to go much more smoothly. It does not require from the individual anything comparable to personal initiative; it is a strictly predetermined development, to a large degree independent of external influences.

In this perspective the whole development, from the moment of impregnation until death, can be divided into two major portions—one before and one after birth. The one before birth accomplishes the development to the point where the individual becomes biologically more or less independent of the mother organism; it can take care of its oxygen consumption alone through respiration and it has the organs through the activity of which it can incorporate the necessary nourishing substances, all of which before birth were supplied by the mother organism. With this biological equipment after birth, it has to solve the second problem, the problem of social adjustment. Biologically seen, this consists first of all in the further development of the central nervous system, the biological basis of the personality. This social adjustment necessarily consists of gradual changes in the function of the finer structures of the central nervous system. These continuous changes, in their details unfortunately almost entirely unknown as yet, develop under the influence of the social environment upon the individual; physiologically seen, they are the results of the stimuli of the environment upon the sensory organs of the individual in the form mainly of optical and acoustical perceptions, among which stimuli represented by speech take probably the most important place.

It would be unscientific to postulate a fundamental difference between the prenatal portion of the growth of the individual, which we can describe in anatomical and physiological terms, and the postnatal personality development, which at present we can better describe in psychological and sociological terms. Both the prenatal embryological and the postnatal personality development consist of the biological growth and development of the same organism and necessarily are connected with anatomical and physiological changes in the organism. Thanks to Freud's discovery of the psychoanalytic technique, we have recently become able to describe and understand in scientific terms the postnatal portion of this development, which up to that time had been an entirely blank spot on the map of our knowledge. These discoveries developed to a high degree independently of the biological knowledge of the development of the body. It is obvious that the next step will consist in bridging over this gap, in connecting with each other into one entity these two aspects of the development of the human organism, the psychological aspect with the biological. This will be accomplished if the processes of social adjustment are also understood and described in biological terms.

Only the first beginnings have been made in this fundamental problem of interrelating biological and psychological development. In recent years it has become evident to us that the most promising approach to establishing this interrelationship is offered by the study of that very early period of postnatal development in which phylogenetically predetermined processes overlap with personality development in the social sense. New scientific progress usually takes place in such borderline fields. It is only very roughly correct to make a strict distinction between the intrauterine and the extra-uterine phase of development by characterizing the first as automatically and strictly biologically predetermined and the second as more flexible, changeable through external influences, and biologically not predetermined. The biologically predetermined course of development by no means ends with birth. The new-born organism cannot at all be considered as a finished product which is capable of satisfying its biological needs independently. The new-born baby, though anatomically separated from the mother organism, is still biologically dependent on the bodily product of the mother organism, on milk, not to speak of the fact that in order to remain in life it requires the care of the mother in many ways.

Apart from adjustment to the restrictions of social life, there is an important series of organic changes to which the infant's personality has to adjust itself. Even after birth quite a number of phylogenetically predetermined changes take place automatically. Examples are dentition and the change from passive locomotion to active locomotion through learning to walk, which is dependent on biological maturation. Even control of the sphincter functions occurs to a certain degree automatically, though with the help of the environment. The development of the intellectual functions also must be considered to a high degree a predetermined process, although in its detail it is extremely dependent upon environmental influences. Fundamentally it is a biologically determined process which in some way or other would take place with or without specific cultural influences. I speak here only of such basic phases of intellectual development as the increasing faculty of differentiating between objects, the increasing precision of the reality-testing function, the capacity to make abstractions in the form of conscious thinking. All these increased capacities are based on the development of certain higher centers of the brain.

Even as late as in adolescence a biologically predetermined change takes place in the organism, a change of the utmost importance for personality development—the maturation of the sex glands, and with it the capacity for propagation. After sexual maturity follow senescence and death, the last phases of the life history, which are equally biologically conditioned.

The psychoanalytic study of neurotic and psychotic individuals has more and more focused our attention upon those early periods of personality development after birth in which the individual still has to solve fundamental problems of a biological, not a cultural, nature. During this early period the individual becomes entirely independent of the mother organism in his nutrition and locomotion, and learns also to control his excretory functions. Our studies have shown that during this early period the instinctive cravings of the individual undergo very profound changes. We call this portion of the development the pregenital or pre-Œdipal period. The study of this pre-Œdipal period is possible by applying the analytical technique to neurotic and psychotic adults. In such individuals there is a strong regressive tendency to return to the early forms of emotional expression. This regressive tendency becomes especially active if the neurotic is exposed to emotional difficulties and conflicts during the process of his adjustment. Every neurotic symptom can be considered as such a regression of the patient to early forms of instinctive gratification, to emotional attitudes in which he felt still happy and contented. This regressive nature of neurotic and psychotic symptoms gives us a great opportunity to study the early forms of emotional and instinctive life.

Recently these more indirect studies of the early phases of emotional development in neurotic adults have been complemented in a most instructive way by direct observation of the child through the technique of child-analysis. Both of these types of study have shown us that this pre-Œdipal period of development has the greatest significance for the later personality development; in fact, it is this early phase in which the basic character trends are formed. These studies have shown us, furthermore, that during this early period the child goes through emotional changes which are incomparably deeper and more significant than anything that takes place later in its life.

In essence the problem that the child's personality has to solve during this phase is also a problem of adjustment, but in the first place it is an adjustment to the phylogenetically predetermined sequence of changes in its biological status. It is the inexorable fate of this little helpless being to become gradually more and more independent. Study of the unconscious shows us clearly the powerful emotional protest in the child against this separation from the mother, a protest against every step in the direction of independence. From the psychology of the conscious mental life we know only the progressive drive, the wish to grow up, the ambition to excel and be successful, but study of the unconscious reveals underneath a powerful opposing tendency to regress to the earlier period of dependence in which there is no responsibility and in which one is fully taken care of by the parents.

In this early period the cravings of the individual are not yet connected with elaborate ideational content; they are general emotional cravings connected with the biological functions of the organism. They center around nutrition associated with pleasure sensations in the mouth: to receive, to incorporate, is the content of these cravings and satisfactions. Another emotional tendency which seemingly becomes emotionally charged somewhat later than the incorporating tendencies is related to the eliminating functions. The eliminating tendencies and the pleasure sensations involved in the process of excretion are mixed with retentive tendencies and pleasure sensations resulting from the retention of bodily products. *Incorporation, elimination,* and *retention* are those general tendencies around which the emotional life of the child revolves.

One may say that in this early period the child's emotional universe expresses an entirely vegetative philosophy of life, and emotional relationships to persons play as yet an unimportant rôle. The pleasure sensations are located at this time in the organs of nutrition and elimination and are connected with their functions.

This picture gradually changes, and between the third and sixth year the child develops more and more personal emotional relationships with individuals, and during the same time the pleasure sensations from the vegetative organs gradually become transferred to the genitals. It is a most significant parallelism that the development of emotional object relationships coincides with the first signs of sexual maturation. But only seven or eight years later, in adolescence, does the individual achieve full genital maturity and become capable of propagation. This long period interpolated between the first manifestations of genitality and full genital maturity is typical for the human animal, and so far as I know is unparalleled in the animal world. The origin and significance of this phenomenon is still an open field for speculation.

The achievement of sexual maturity divides the life of the individual into two fundamentally different phases. Before sexual maturity, the individual is essentially a child, is engaged in the process of growth, and in many respects is dependent and receptive toward the parents. After sexual maturation the process of growth is terminated; the individual becomes capable of reproduction and responsible for the support of the next generation. He stops being a child and is capable of having children. The period of emotional dependence ends. To incorporation and retention in order to grow, and to the elimination of waste substances, a new form of elimination is added, a creative function, the production of germ cells, and through that the creation of new life with all the responsibilities and energy expenditures which the support of the new generation involves. Parallel with this biological change, a new emotional tendency becomes of central importance, the tendency to give.

Propagation can be considered biologically as

growth beyond the limits of the individual organism. In the monocellular organism this is easily observable. It grows, and after it reaches a certain limit of growth it divides itself into two parts and dies, or at least stops existing as an individual, but continues to live in the two new organisms that have been formed from it. In the polycellular organism fundamentally the same process takes place, the only difference being that propagation consists of an asymmetrical division, and the parent organism continues to live its own life for a while after reproduction.

Psychoanalysis of normal adults shows that not only in neurotics and psychotics but in everyone there is a strong regressive tendency opposing this progressive course of development, which starts with total dependence upon the mother organism and leads, after the achievement of full sexual maturity, to death. Every external difficulty which the individual encounters during the course of this progressive development contributes to this inner regressive force throwing him back to the earlier infantile forms of emotional expression. External difficulties leading to fear, deprivation, failure in life have a powerful internal ally in the regressive tendencies of the organism. In neurotics and especially in psychotics this regressive tendency is greatly accentuated, and even very small defeats in the first love relationships, slight disappointments and rejections, are used as a good excuse to give in to the unconscious regressive trends, to the wish to give up the fight for independence, to give up the object relationships, and to retreat to the early vegetative forms of emotional life centering around the individual himself—which leads to the egocentric existence so typical of the mentally and emotionally disturbed patient. In many cases, especially in certain schizophrenics, the traumatic experiences in life seem to be really only secondary precipitating causes, excuses to give in to the regressive trend. The real etiological factor is the strong fixation and regression to the dependent phases of the development in which the individual had as yet no responsibilities and was fully taken care of by the parents.

This unwillingness to grow up and to accept the emotional attitude that corresponds to the biological status of maturity in many cases seems to be the most important etiological factor. Especially in cases of schizophrenic psychosis, this endogenous regressive tendency, a certain inertia or rigidity of the instinctive life, an unwillingness to pass through the different phases of development in the direction of maturity, is the most important factor, and the external traumatic experiences are of only secondary significance. They *push* back the individual in the direction of infancy toward which his fixation and powerful regressive tendencies tend to *pull* him back. Whether this strong regressive tendency of the instinctive life characteristic of psychotics is, as Freud assumes, of a congenital nature or is acquired during the very early phases of the postnatal development is as yet undecided.

It seems, however, that at least in many cases of psychosis the inflexibility of the instinctive life, the exaggerated resistance against growing up emotionally, is an inherited, constitutional quality. In these cases, even thorough etiological studies are unable to discover extremely pathogenetic traumatic life experiences, at least no more violent ones than the usual emotional conflicts that are common also in the life history of normal and psychoneurotic individuals. On the other hand, in the early history of many schizophrenics, from the beginnings of the extra-uterine life one sees a peculiar and stubborn refusal of the baby to accept the consecutive changes in its biological situation. They often show an unusually strong dependence upon the mother and react to the first social contacts with withdrawal, shyness, and anxiety. Later in life they react to slight deprivations and failures with disproportionate intensity, and to every difficulty their reaction is withdrawal and flight.

This magnetic attraction back to the early infantile situation which we observe in the psychotic in such an exaggerated form, in somewhat less intensive form in neurotics, and even less in normals, is nevertheless a universal phenomenon of the emotional life.

We see that the history of emotional development has certain universal features which are phylogenetically predetermined and which are the psychological reflection of the chain of biological events that start with the total dependence of the organism in the intra-uterine situation and lead through birth to an increasing independence, then to sexual maturation and reproduction, and finally to involution and death. The emotional development in its main features follows strictly these predetermined phases and sequences of biological development. The dependent, receptive, emotional attitude of the infant is the expression of its dependent biological situation just as much as the self-assurance and the productive and creative tendencies of the healthy adult are an expression of his sexual maturity, and the contemplative acquiescence of the healthy old man is the expression of his biological involution, to which he has adjusted himself emotionally.

Another example of adjustment to the unchangeable facts of biological fate has been recently described by Freud in female development. Freud advanced the theory that the abandonment by the little girl of her early masculine aspirations resulting from her biologically determined bisexuality is an emotional adjustment which follows the discovery that, because of her anatomical structure, these masculine strivings are doomed to frustration.

In its early years psychoanalysis impressed upon us the importance of the adjustment of the instinctive cravings to the social milieu, to the restrictions that collective life requires; recently more and more we are beginning to realize that the personality has also to adjust itself to an even more inescapable environment than the external social environment—namely, to the ever-changing inner environment represented by the biologically conditioned changes of its instinctive cravings. Analytic studies show that perhaps the greatest emotional difficulty that the human being has to solve during his life is the relinquishment of the biological dependence upon the mother and the acceptance of the mature emotional attitude which corresponds to the status of biological maturity.

The picture offered us by the microscopic study of life histories with the magnifying glass of psychoanalytic technique is as if the individual would accept only reluctantly the independent state of maturity, driven to it by the inexorable course of biological growth; and as if deep down it never would renounce fully the longing to return to the happiness of the irresponsible dependence of infancy. The mythology of the golden age and especially the Biblical story of *Genesis,* of the Garden of Eden, are clear testimonies of this regressive craving of man for the lost paradise of childhood, from which he was expelled after he had eaten from the tree of sexual knowledge. The Biblical story of expulsion betrays an intuitive grasp of the fact that the achievement of sexual maturity is the critical turning point in life, which ends the careless vegetative phase of dependence. *"Noblesse oblige!"* Every new biological capacity acquired during development means a new obligation for the individual: After he develops teeth, he loses the right to be nursed at the breast; after he learns to walk, he loses the right to be carried around; and after he achieves the capacity of producing children, he loses the right to be a child.

Unquestionably the external cultural environment begins very early to exert an influence and modifies this development in its details. Different ideologies, habits, and customs reflect themselves in the customs of the family, in the philosophy and technique of bringing up the children. Different cultural attitudes of the parents to the children may influence the process of emotional maturation to a high degree. But there is a fundamental universal scheme of emotional development which every individual has to pass through under the pressure of the unchangeable facts of biological growth and involution. Just as in a symphony there is a ground-motif running through all the variations, so also in a life history one recognizes behind the secondary influences of the cultural environment the deep, powerful groundwork of the biological determinants.

In order to understand personality development and evaluate the effect of cultural influences upon it, it is most important to know this universal, biologically determined ground plan which can be only secondarily modified and changed through external cultural influences. It is evident that the emotional development of the early phases is much more uniform and rigidly predetermined than the later fate of the individual. In many respects the first period of development is still a continuation of the embryological development, a completion of it according to phylogenetically predetermined patterns. Yet at the same time in this early period the organism can be already considered also as a personality which reacts emotionally to these automatic changes in its biological status. That is why, as I mentioned before, the study of this early phase is so promising for the understanding of psycho-biological interrelationships. The content of these early emotional reactions is still so closely related to the fundamental biological processes of incorporation, elimination, and retention that they can be considered as the elementary tendencies from which the abundant variety of the later psychological life develops.

The latest stage of psychoanalysis is characterized by the increased attention paid to these early phases of personality development. The practical significance of these studies consists in allowing us a new approach for the understanding and treating of certain emotionally conditioned organic disturbances. In such cases very deep regressions to this early pregenital or vegetative phase of the emotional life have taken place. These regressive tendencies constitute an emotional over-charge of organic functions—functions that in normal cases take place automatically without much interference from the emotional life.

We may hope that another practical significance of the study of these early periods of emotional life will be the better understanding of the psychological meaning of psychoses in which, as I have mentioned, deep emotional regressions to early phases of life play such an important rôle.

It is to be expected that the study of these early emotional reactions will also be of great significance in the clarification of the problems of inherited constitution, which is so much needed at the present time. The earlier the manifestations we can study, the better shall we be able to isolate general dynamic trends that are as yet uninfluenced by external factors and must, therefore, be considered as inherited.

Finally the study of the interrelationship of the biologically determined ground plan of emotional development with its secondary modifications and distortions by external cultural influences will bring us nearer to the ultimate goal—to a complete understanding of man as an organism, as a personality, and as a member of a social group.

V.

Psychic Influences on Body Functions

General Remarks

STRONG and independent minds are needed to make progress against dogmatic opposition. It is a curious coincidence that the scientific revolution against the one-sided mechanistic medicine of the late nineteenth century happened to start in Vienna, the strongest center of the best laboratory tradition. The first move, however, came from France. Freud, a pupil of Brücke, the Viennese physiologist, and Meynert, the brain anatomist, was wholly dominated by the anatomical point of view when he first came to Paris to attend the lectures of Charcot (1887). Charcot was an empiricist in the best sense of the word. His great reverence for facts enabled him to emancipate himself from the prevailing dogmatic theories which gave no place to psychological factors in the causation of pathological processes. After he had learned that hysterical symptoms, like the paresis of one arm, can arise under the influence of certain ideas, he succeeded in reproducing hysterical symptoms experimentally by the help of suggestions which he made to patients under hypnosis. These experiments have proved conclusively that psychological factors such as ideas can disturb the functions of organs morphologically intact. Hypnosis, having been introduced by an authority like Charcot, became a legitimate method of research, although in the minds of many physicians it is associated even today with medieval black magic, rather than with modern medicine. It does not suit modern medicine, which has more and more assumed the exterior of physics and chemistry, in which the technical instrument has undertaken leadership. Nevertheless, experiments in hypnosis by competent and critical investigators have resulted in the accumulation of a vast collection of facts which show that even the functions of those organs that work automatically and have no apparent connection with ordinary mental life can be influenced by hypnotic suggestions. Most extraordinary has appeared the fact that even organs, the functions of which are not subject to conscious will, could be influenced by the hypnotist's commands; for example, the frequency of the heart contractions, or the blood supply of certain organs through circumscribed contraction of the capillaries, or the function of the sudoriferous glands. It would seem that some of the unverified statements about Indian yogis, who by long and strenuous training voluntarily control physiological processes that are normally automatic, might be confirmed.

The Relation of the Autonomic Nervous System to the Central Nervous System

I must confess that I have never been able to explain satisfactorily the stubborn resistance which modern medicine maintains in the face of clinical and experimental proofs against the assumption of psychogenic disturbances of the organs, the functions of which are regulated by the autonomic nervous system. The connection of the cortex with the visceral organs through the sympathetic and para-sympathetic system is sufficiently well known, and this connection implies that essentially every peripheral physiological process, in whatever part of the body it takes place, can potentially be influenced by psychological factors. The mere fact that most organic functions are automatic and seemingly independent of psychological influences does not imply that under certain conditions cortical, *i.e.*, psychological influences, cannot take place. There are, moreover, certain biological considerations which justify the assumption that voluntary innervations represent the primary form of motor innervation and that reflexes and automatic functions are products of a secondary development. We know that many reflectory or automatic functions are acquired, *i.e.*, learned during the individual's lifetime. The adjustment of the organism to the environment consists chiefly in the automatization of those behavior patterns which prove to be the most suitable. To mention only one well-known phenomenon, when a child learns to walk, he at first makes groping attempts at locomotion and ends by performing what is almost an automatic function. It is true that walking, though automatic, remains subject to the conscious will, so that we can change the speed and length of our steps and consciously start and stop walking. The automatic functions of visceral organs, on the other hand, are usually inaccessible to voluntary interference, even though in unusual states like hypnosis influence by suggestion is possible. The question arises whether it is justifiable to consider this unusual voluntary influence as a reëstablishment of an archaic faculty, which has been lost in the course of phylogenetic development.

Phylogenetic considerations make it seem probable that the automatic regulation of organic functions is a secondary process and that the original behavior of the living protoplasm is a groping and voluntary motor innervation, such as we see in the behavior of monocellular organisms. If I use the expression "voluntary" in this case, it is only because we have no other term for the primitive equivalent of psychological impulses in primitive beings corresponding to the conscious will of highly developed organisms. That psychological impulses cannot be regarded as the privilege of the higher vertebrates, or as dependent upon a certain stage in the biological development, is so obvious a philosophical postulate that its further discussion is superfluous.

In primitive monocellular organisms, even the vegetative functions are not yet consolidated, and organs such as the arm and mouth are created *ad hoc* only for the moment and disappear after their function has been fulfilled in conformity with the undifferentiated protoplasmic body. Thus the body and its different organs can be considered as structuralized and solidified functions or, in other words, the function is the formative factor and is responsible for the morphological structure.[1] The differentiation and automatization of the vegetative organ functions is a long process of the adjustment of the race to the biological processes which the organisms have to solve, and the differentiation of the so-called autonomic nervous system which regulates the functions of the

[1] Dr. G. Zilboorg has called my attention to the behavior of the monocellular beings as the best illustration of the dynamic creations of organs.

vegetative organs has to be considered as a secondary process. The original biological structure was a uniform nervous control which had the task both of orientation to the external world and the regulation of inner processes. The development of an autonomic nervous system which is to a certain degree independent of the central nervous system is a product of development and serves to unburden the central nervous system of part of its work. This division of labor, in coping with the two fundamental problems of the organism, the orientation in the external world and the regulation of the inner processes, increases the efficiency of the organism. The central nervous system, relieved of the task of inner regulation, becomes more efficient in solving the problems of orientation in external reality. An entire independence of the autonomic nervous system from the central nervous system is, however, not realized in the human body. There is a complicated interrelation between the autonomic ganglia and the central nervous system, and all visceral organs receive nerve fibres both from central origin and from sympathetic ganglia which lie outside the central nervous system. Therefore the concept of the autonomic nervous system is much more functional than anatomical, because morphologically they are closely interrelated and the innervation of the inner organs is always mixed.

Dr. Edward G. Kempf in his book, "The Autonomic Functions and the Personality," [1] comes to a
seemingly entirely opposite conclusion, namely, that
the autonomic nervous system is the primary structure
around which the cerebro-spinal system has been con-
structed in the course of development. Dealing with
this problem, however, one has to separate two distinct questions: (1) the relation of the two basic
functions of the organism, the regulation of the vegetative functions (inner affairs of the organism), and
the orientation in the environment (external affairs)
(2) the question of the *kind* of nervous control, *i.e.*,
central (voluntary) and autonomic (involuntary)
nervous control. Kempf evidently deals with the first
question in making the assumption that the nervous
control of the vegetative functions, *i.e.*, the internal
affairs of the organism, is organized first and that the
orientation and reactions to the external environment
by the help of a "proficient sensory-motor system" is
a secondary process. We are not, however, concerned
here with the problem of whether the nervous control
of the vegetative functions or that of the orientation
in the environment has developed earlier; but we ask
only which *kind* of nervous control, the central or
autonomic, is primary. My assumption is that at an

[1] Edward G. Kempf: "The Autonomic Functions and the Personality," *Nervous and Mental Diseases Monograph Series*, No. 28,
Washington, 1918.

early stage of development probably both the vegetative functions and the orientation in the environment were not yet anatomically differentiated but controlled by a single central system. The morphological manifestation of the later differentiation would be, according to this concept, the peripheral migration of the sympathetic ganglia. Embryological studies have shown that originally the sympathetic motor (excitor) cells lie within the central nervous system close up to the posterior root ganglia and that only later do they migrate outwards peripherally.[1] Thus the morphological separation of the autonomic and central nervous systems, which is—to be sure—not a complete separation, is a result of development. Also, Kempf assumes that the differentiation of both systems progresses during development. But it is meaningless, it seems to me, to speak of an autonomic system before a central system has been established, since autonomy implies a central government from which certain functions are separated and carried out more or less independent of the central control. The question is whether or not the autonomic nervous control of the vegetative functions—partially separated as it is both functionally and morphologically from the central system—is a result of later

---

[1] Samson Wright: *Applied Physiology,* p. 95. Oxford Medical Publications, Humphrey Milford, London, 1926.

differentiation. That the need for autonomy in all kinds of organizations arises later in development when the central control becomes too complex is a general principle of biological development. The question whether Kempf's theory of the primacy of the nervous control of the vegetative functions, to which he really refers in his developmental theory, is justified or not lies outside the scope of this book.

The question whether the autonomic nervous system can be considered as a differentiated product of the central nervous system can be finally decided only by embryological investigation. Although the origin of the autonomic ganglia is not yet entirely clear, the major part of their neurons seems to develop from the ventral (motor) part of the neural tube. But it is not finally established whether the cells which become differentiated into autonomic neurons actually descend from the cerebro-spinal nervous system. According to the theory of Schaper,[1] they come from so-called "indifferent" cells which produce the specific cell elements of the nervous system. On the other hand, if one considers the fact that the ganglia of the sympathetic trunks are commonly regarded as efferent

[1] A. Schaper: "Die frühesten Differenzierungsvorgänge im Zentralnervensystem. Kritische Studie und Versuch einer Geschichte der Entwickelung nervöser Substanz." *Arch. f. Entw.-Mech.*, 5, 81-132. (Quoted from *The Autonomic Nervous System*, by Albert Kuntz, p. 521. Lea & Febiger, Philadelphia, 1929.)

(motor) in function ("excitor cells"), one cannot escape the impression that the extra cerebro-spinal autonomic centers are peripherally displaced motor centers.[1] This displacement is the manifestation of the physiological tendency to give internal organs an increasingly higher grade of motor autonomy. The only real autonomic functions are those of the peripheral ganglia of the heart and the submucous ganglia of the intestinal canal. Naturally these organs are at the same time subject to central influences through the sympathetic and the para-sympathetic nervous system. Further embryological study of the origin of the autonomic ganglia would be of the highest theoretical value.

Thus both psychological and somatic considerations support the assumption that neurotic mechanisms, in which organs with automatic regulations are influenced by psychological motives, are archaic processes in which the organism regresses to a state in which all organic functions still were in closer connection with emotional life.

[1] For example, J. B. Johnston considers it entirely settled that the sympathetic system is a developmental product of the central nervous system in stating that, regardless of some unsettled theoretical questions as to the origin of the sympathetic neurons, "it should be held clearly in mind that the sympathetic system is an offshoot or subsidiary portion of the visceral afferent and efferent divisions of the nervous system which has come to have a special structure and arrangement owing to the conditions of the visceral activities." J. B. Johnston: *The Nervous System of Vertebrates*, p. 216, P. Blakiston's Son & Co., Philadelphia, 1906.

We can, however, entirely disregard the question of the phylogenetic primacy of central and autonomic innervations, and it remains a fact that the major part of our biological accomplishments consists in expressing and satisfying psychological needs, wishes and emotions, through motor innervations, no matter whether this physical expression of psychic facts consists in complicated movements of our extremities in carrying out the tasks of everyday life, or whether melancholy ideas influence the secretion of the lachrymal sac, or whether under the influence of strong emotions, such as pleasure or fear, our heart begins to beat more rapidly, our cheeks become red or pale, and at the same time the distribution of the blood supply is probably changed in all the organs.

Apart from these generally known psychomotor reactions of everyday life such as weeping, laughter, blushing, panting in fear, sighing of despair or relief, and palpitation in fright, recent laboratory studies have revealed a series of formerly unknown bodily reactions to psychic stimuli. Among these the most significant are Cannon's experiments on animals, demonstrating the influence of fear and rage upon the adrenal system. In animals fear and rage stimulate the production of adrenalin, which in turn mobilizes the carbohydrate depots and supplies the attacked animal in its emergency situation with this source of chemical energy, easily convertible into mechanical energy. The significance of this discovery lies in the fact that it demonstrates the influence of emotional factors upon the whole energy household of the organisms, upon the most fundamental process of life: on metabolism.

Analysis of Psychic Factors

It can easily be shown, however, that even the most common psychomotor processes cannot be satisfactorily described without the precise knowledge of psychic factors. As an example the process of weeping or laughing may be considered, both of which are based on complicated psychomotor reflexes. A statement that sad ideas are able to influence the function of the lachrymal glands is a vague generality, the scientific uselessness of which becomes clear from the following imaginary experiment. The problem is to establish those conditions under which the physiological process of weeping is provoked in different individuals. Let it be assumed that to solve this problem a hundred individuals are exposed to a moving picture. It will then be observed that by a certain touching scene a certain percentage of the hundred are unable to control their tears and react with the unsuccessful suppression of sobbing, whereas another group are much less touched and a third group remain entirely cold and observe the plot critically without any emotional participation in it. It would be, however, entirely false to jump from these differences of reaction to the conclusion that the persons who remained cold are less sentimental in general, because a second experiment will prove that, confronted with another scene on the screen, a great percentage of those who remained undisturbed by the first scene will now react with intensive sobbing and crying. If this kind of observation in exposing the experimental individuals to different scenes is patiently followed up, it may be possible to distinguish certain specific situations to which certain groups of individuals react with weeping, and the specific sensitiveness of certain individuals to certain situations might even be considered as a characteristic feature of them that they acquired under the influence of their former experiences.

This thorough analysis of psychic processes is made possible by the psychoanalytic technique. By this method it becomes possible to answer the question encountered in the former experiment, namely, why certain individuals are especially sensitive to certain situations.

Psychogenic Disturbances

In spite of the predominantly physicochemical orientation of modern medicine, in his everyday practice the physician is permanently reminded of the significance of emotional factors in the causation of organic disturbances; in fact, he is more often consulted by patients who suffer "only" from a nervous stomach, or a nervous palpitation, or from some intestinal trouble of obscure etiology (diarrhoea-constipation), in which emotional factors are obviously involved, than by patients suffering from purely organic ailment, that the physician can explain and cure on an entirely physiological basis. In dealing with such psychogenic cases the general practitioner usually is satisfied with eliminating a serious organic condition. He considers such cases to belong rather to medical art than to medical science.

When the organic origin of the symptom has been carefully eliminated and when at the same time the patient's manifest behavior exhibits what is commonly called nervousness, then, and only then, the physician feels justified in assuming psychic factors. After such a diagnosis has been made and expressed in vague terms taken from everyday language, such as "nervous exhaustion," "unstable personality" or "fatigue from overwork," or by the eclectic use of old and new technical terms such as "neurasthenia," "psychasthenia," "psychopathy" and other more or less indefinite expressions, the physician feels himself prepared to give therapeutic advice. The general notion is that the patient's nervous system is somehow over-taxed by the emotional strain of worries, fears, manifest discontent with life as it is, or by simply too much responsibility or overwork. There is little inclination to go more deeply into the nature of the patient's psychological situation.

In the field of pathology, however, just as in the case of psychomotor phenomena of everyday life, it is unsatisfactory to accept general phrases—for example, saying that the stomach symptoms of a patient are based on his nervousness and are provoked by steady excitements. Such an explanation is exactly as empty as the one that weeping is caused by sad ideas. A psychogenic stomach trouble is based on just as specific psychic processes as weeping or laughing or blushing. Here again it is necessary to establish the specific psychic process that is responsible for the stomach symptoms. Only such a detailed insight into the totality of a psychophysiological process allows a real causal therapy.

The Dual Personality of the Modern Physician

Thus modern clinical medicine appears to consist of two heterogeneous portions: A portion considered more advanced and scientific including all disturbances which are understood in terms of physiology and general pathology (for example, organic heart defects, diabetes, infectious diseases, etc.), and a less highly regarded unscientific chapter including the great conglomeration of ailments of obscure, frequently psychic origin. Characteristic of this attitude—a typical manifestation of the inertia of the human mind—is the tendency to force more and more diseases into the etiological scheme of infection, where pathogenic cause and pathological effect appear to have a comparatively simple relationship with each other. When the infectious or some other organic explanation fails the modern clinician is only too ready to console himself with the hope that some time in the future, after more details of the organic processes will be known, the so unwillingly admitted psychic factor will be eventually eliminated. And yet, gradually more and more clinicians with a broader perspective come to recognize that even in physiologically well understood disturbances such as diabetes or essential hypertension only the last links in the causal chain are known and the primary etiological factors still remain in the dark. In these, as in other chronic conditions, accumulated observations seem to point to a "central" origin, the expression "central" being obviously merely a euphemism for "psychogenic."

This state of affairs easily explains the peculiar discrepancy between the official-theoretical and the factual-practical attitude of the physician in his practice. In his scientific contributions, in his addresses to medical groups, he will exclusively stress the need for knowing more and more details about the underlying physiological and pathological processes, and he will refuse to believe seriously any psychogenic etiology; in his private practice, however, he will without hesitation advise his patient suffering from an essential hypertension to try to relax, take life less seriously, avoid overwork, eliminate worries from his life, and he will try to convince his patient that his over-active, over-ambitious attitude in life is the real source of his high blood pressure. This "dual personality" of the modern clinician indeed reveals more clearly than anything else the weak spot of present-day medicine. Within the medical community the practitioner can afford to assume a "scientific," in fact only a dogmatic anti-psychological attitude, but confronted with his patients his therapeutic conscience forces him to pay primary attention to the detested psychic factor, the importance of which he instinctively senses; yet because he does not know exactly how this psychic element works, and because it is so contradictory to everything he learned during his medical training, and because the recognition of the psychic factor seemingly disrupts the consistency of the physicochemical theory of life, he tries to disregard it as much as possible. As a practitioner, however, he cannot entirely avoid dealing with the psychic factor, he must consider it, but in doing so he excuses himself with the phrase that medical healing is not only science but also art. At the same time he does not notice that what he refers to as medical art is nothing but his deeper intuitive, *i.e.*, his not verbalized knowledge that he obtained during the long years of clinical experience.

It is obvious that this obscure field will become more scientific by a more precise knowledge of the "psychic factor," and not by the futile attempts to deny it or reduce it to hypothetical physiological processes.

Probably the great significance of psychoanalysis for the future development of medicine lies in its capacity to supply an efficient technique for the study of the "psychic factor."

VI.

Recognition of Psychic Factors in Modern Medicine

General Remarks

THE superiority of analytic psychology in describing and explaining the details of psychopathological processes made it inevitable that its influence on modern psychiatry should ultimately be felt. The relations between psychoanalysis and general medicine, however, were much slower in developing. The discrepancy between the official medical attitude toward psychoanalysis and its actual rôle in general practice is becoming daily more obvious. While the medical schools officially regard psychoanalysis as a persistent but passing fad, or as a questionable and highly speculative system, not yet and probably never ripe for use in medicine, the general practitioner usually knows something about it and is influenced by it in his daily work. His knowledge, however, was not obtained at the medical schools or universities but is intuitive or is gained from hearsay, and thus the paradoxical situation has arisen in the last two decades that although medical authorities officially do not take notice of psychoanalysis, there is a tendency in medical practice which might be called "psychologism." It is, however, impossible for knowledge acquired in so haphazard and unsystematic a manner to be sound, critical and well-balanced. It exhibits all manner of impurities and in general the practitioner has been the victim rather than the master of the situation. While some years ago psychogenic factors were considered mythical concepts which had no place in an exact science, very recently the opposite attitude is characteristic of many modern practitioners, who like to detect psychogenic causes for everything. Not long ago, a physician had to be reminded that his patient had a personality and a mental life with difficult and important conflicts, but now some physicians must be reminded that besides mental problems there is also the complicated machinery of the body to be reckoned with. It is impossible to deny that the dogmatic attitude of the medical schools is responsible for this uncritical, pan-psychological attitude, which is nothing but an exaggerated reaction against the preceding un-psychological period in medicine which refused to take notice of Freud's new science.

In 1930–1931 I was invited to teach Psychoanalysis in the University of Chicago and had ample opportunity to study the different attitudes of my medical colleagues toward this first attempt to bring psychoanalysis into contact with other medical disciplines. Their reactions appeared variously in stubborn refusal to take any notice of it, in prejudiced attacks, in open-minded but critical interest, and in enthusiastic coöperation. I cannot, therefore, agree with those analysts who are impatient or bitter about the resistance which psychoanalysis meets in medicine and who give up trying to convince their critics and retire to splendid isolation, content with the feeling that they know more about human nature than their stubborn antagonists. I do not think that they have any right to complain of the opposition to psychoanalysis, for it is a typical, unavoidable phenomenon in the development of every science and has appeared repeatedly even in the brief history of scientific medicine whenever an important fundamental discovery has been made.

A few sketchy historical considerations may serve to explain the unstable position of psychoanalysis, which has become one of the most awkward problems of contemporary medical teaching and administration as well as a question of cardinal importance in medical and biological research. An examination of the situation from a detached historical point of view results in the impression that the appearance of psychoanalysis on the scientific scene is accompanied by all the signs of those rare moments when important scientific revolutions start. Psychoanalysis does not impress us merely as an important new method or as an isolated discovery, but as the beginning of a new phase in biological and medical thinking. Only its fundamental significance can explain the violent resistance it has evoked.

Earlier Views of the Psychogenesis of Organic Diseases

The neglect of psychological facts, especially of the mental state of the patient, has not always been as prevalent in medicine as in the period from the middle of the last century up to the present. In the pre-scientific period, which may also be called the "pre-laboratory period," when medicine was more of an art than a science and was based more on intuition and on general rather than detailed empirical observations, the physician laid a much greater stress on the psychological state of the patient and attempted to explain disease not only as the consequence of pathological changes in the different organs, but as the consequence of the conditions of his whole life. In those days it was easy for the physician not to be one-sided and to consider all the pathological phenomena because he knew very few details, especially of the finer biological processes.

An echo of this attitude is found in the literature of those days which, for example, presented tuberculosis in a romantic fashion as a consequence of great mental catastrophes, which led to flight from a life already judged worthless. In the course of time the bacillus tuberculosis was discovered, and the natural effect of this was to regard all kinds of psychogenic etiological explanations as popular superstitions. Only quite recently has it been reaffirmed that a full etiological account even of an infectious disease like tuberculosis, which is caused by a highly specific microörganism, must reckon with psychological factors. Statistical investigation has proved that there is striking discrepancy between the amount of actual infection by Koch's bacillus and florid cases of tuberculosis. In view of the omnipresence of the bacillus tuberculosis in the great industrial centers, it has become a most interesting problem to discover the variable factors responsible for the fact that only a fraction of the persons infected becomes actually sick. In addition to constitution and acquired immunity, it has been necessary to assume that the psychological state of the individual exposed to infection is also a factor in his resistance to the disease. This is only one example of the recent change; credit is once more given to the old empirical observation of the influence of psychological factors in disease.

No matter how important and correct this new psychological aspect, the evaluation of the patient's psychic condition, might be, it is easy to understand that the necessity of introducing this unknown and intangible factor was bound to annoy and discourage the modern physician. The patient's "psychological condition" is indeed an etiological concept which is not on the same scientific level as that of a well-defined microörganism or of the more or less measurable amount of the body's immunity against an infection. While the latter belong to the familiar field of natural science, the introduction of psychological factors was like a slap in the face to the biologically oriented physician, who was reminded of those days not long past when medicine was a branch of sorcery and therapy a form of exorcism. Scientific medicine is still young and only recently recognized as an exact natural science and is, therefore, particularly sensitive to the introduction of psychological concepts which appear similar to the animistic theories in which it was once entangled. The invasion of medicine by psychology is felt by the majority as introducing an unknown factor, incapable of tangible and scientific definition and approach. The idea that the patient's "mental condition" may influence well defined physicochemical processes is too general a notion to be considered seriously, and even if it be described more specifically as nervousness, worry, or chronic fear and apprehension, still the causal connection between these phenomena and the tangible physiological processes is very unsatisfactory.

The fundamental significance of psychoanalysis consists just in filling this gap by replacing psychological generalities like "the patient's mental condition" by well defined, highly specific, empirical and detailed psychological observation. Thus psychoanalysis eliminates the difference of scientific character between psychological and physical facts.

The history of medicine is full of indications that certain connections between psychological and physiological processes were perceived intuitively from general observation even in the pre-scientific period. The majority of these guesses still await a scientific explanation as, for example, the old Galenic conception of the temperaments which has been revived in modern constitutional research, especially in the works of Kretschmer. Old and vague notions of a connection of mental disturbances and glandular functions betray themselves in expressions like "melancholia" (black bile). But it is noteworthy that in this field even the modern clinician can only make general statements, for example, that certain people with a peculiar physical structure, whom Kretschmer called "pyknic" types, exhibit an unexplained inclination toward disturbances in the functions of the great visceral glands and at the same time toward melancholic states. The intimate nature of this coincidence is by no means clarified and we do not know whether it is the result of a third unknown factor or whether the melancholic process is responsible for the pathological functioning of certain glands.

Balzac's *Cousin Pons* is a unique literary document which reflects the medical thinking of its time. It is the story of an odd bachelor, Pons, an eccentric collector of pictures, and a gourmand, who dies of a gall bladder affection, having developed a severe form of melancholia. Cousin Pons is a classical representative of the type of personality later presented by Freud, Abraham, Jones and other psychoanalysts in scientific terms, a case which we psychoanalysts would call a combination of "anal" and "oral" character. He also belongs, according to Kretschmer's classification, to the pyknic type. The novel is nothing but the case history of melancholia with a subsequent gall bladder disturbance which was the last act in the drama of the mental breakdown of this eccentric character. The extraordinary intuition of Balzac has here created an imaginative case history, which a general practitioner, whose experience is not limited to laboratory tests, would call typical.

The life of Pons consisted, apart from collecting antique objects of art, in the satisfaction of his gourmanderie. He was the regular guest of his rich relatives, who belonged to the mondaine society of Paris and who rewarded him with dinner invitations for his expert opinion in purchasing valuable works of art. Once, after an elaborate dinner in the house of a relative, he overheard the servants calling him an old parasite and in that moment saw himself objectively, understood his undignified, senseless existence, and decided never to accept an invitation again. He kept his resolution, retired into seclusion and lived an ascetic, lonesome life. In giving up the visits to his relatives he relinquished the last tie to the external world, and his only form of physical satisfaction. Henceforth the emptiness of his bachelor existence became unbearable and he developed melancholia.

The striking effect of this story on the psychoanalyst can only be understood by knowing that Karl Abraham was able to trace the disposition toward melancholic depressions to a fixation on the early satisfactions of the suckling period.[1] After a masterful presentation of the symptoms of melancholia, Balzac

---

[1] Karl Abraham: *Versuch einer Entwicklungsgeschichte der Libido auf Grund der Psychoanalyse seelischer Storungen,* Internationaler Psychoanalytischer Verlag, Wien, 1924.

has his hero develop a disturbance of the gall bladder which results in his death. The author tries to impress us that the organic illness was the last and necessary consequence of the mental breakdown of Cousin Pons, and we have to admit that the coincidence of the triad—oral fixation, melancholia, and gall bladder affection—agrees with clinical observation.

I mention this masterpiece not to draw any medical conclusions from an invented case history, although it is, like all great products of art, a striking condensation of many detailed observations, a kind of concentrated reality. What I want to illustrate is that, in general medicine, case histories of this kind containing relevant etiological factors belonging to personality development are wholly lacking. Modern case reports are considered complete if they enumerate physical and chemical data, some of which are either not relevant or at least not known to be relevant to the case, and I venture to say that modern case histories in internal medicine are as incomplete in not knowing and not reporting relevant etiological factors connected with personality development, as Balzac's is in not giving the biological facts.

The Resistance Against Psychogenic Factors
in Modern Medicine

I hope that my reference to certain fundamental defects of the modern clinical approach will not be misunderstood. I do not wish to minimize the results of the "laboratory period," which without doubt has been the most brilliant period in the history of medicine, and which in the second part of the last century has made medicine a natural science in the real sense of the word. All progress, however, is necessarily one-sided. The physicochemical orientation in medicine is unquestionably responsible for great progress, but it is also responsible for the complete neglect of the psychological point of view. Its philosophical postulate has been the expectation that, in a not very far distant future, the body and its functions will be understood as a physicochemical machine. The introduction of psychological factors to explain physical processes seemed to contradict this postulate. I do not doubt that the assumption of a complete physicochemical causality of biological processes is correct, but I do not believe that a *knowledge* of the interplay of physiological and psychological processes interferes with it in the least.

The resistance to psychological considerations in contemporary biology is a typical phenomenon in the history of thought. It is the inhibiting power of tradition opposing development. Ernst Mach, the great Austrian physicist and philosopher, a forerunner of dynamic psychology, described this general phenomenon in his classical presentations of the history of thermodynamics and mechanics as the inhibiting influence of "inveterate habits of thought." It is inertia of thinking resisting the adjustment of old ideas to new discoveries. Just as in physics the mechanistic attempt to reduce all physical phenomena to the motions of corpuscula once inhibited the development of more general electro-dynamic concepts, the exclusively physicochemical point of view in medicine interferes with progress in the investigation of psychological processes. It is a paradox of history that the greater the merits of a traditional attitude, the greater is its retarding influence.

It is a natural inclination to stick to ideas which have proved successful and to deny even facts which seem to endanger old and valuable concepts. It is, therefore, not surprising that the successful physicochemical tradition cannot tolerate the introduction of psychological concepts which seem destructive of the exact basis of medicine.

The Contribution of Psychoanalysis to the
Knowledge of Psycho-Somatic Relations

The first beginnings of psychoanalysis go back to
the concept of "conversion hysteria," in which psychological factors cause bodily symptoms; in fact, one of
the first psychoanalytic case histories of Freud, the
case of Dora, is devoted to the explanation of somatic
symptoms from unconscious psychic influences.

Freud's original view of hysterical conversion
has been already described in the second chapter of
this book.[1] The essence of this theory is that every
psychic tendency seeks adequate bodily expression.
The normal way of such expression goes through the
system which is called the conscious ego, which is probably localized anatomically and physiologically in the
cortex. The conscious ego has control over those
muscle innervations which serve to relieve psychic
tendencies that originate from our biological needs.
All our voluntary innervations serve to satisfy these
needs by appropriate activity. There is also a series
of automatic psychomotor phenomena which serves
to express emotional tensions such as weeping, laughing or blushing. If the passage through these normal
channels is blocked, *i.e.,* an emotional tendency is
repressed, an unusual relief comparable to a short
circuit takes place in the form of an unconscious

[1] See pp. 53 to 62.

innervation. This is the hysterical symptom. It gives symbolic expression to the repressed wish or wishful phantasy, and thus serves as a substitute for a voluntary action, which the patient cannot carry out because of its objectionable content.

The main difference between conscious and unconscious innervations is that the latter do not go through the conscious ego. If it is really desired to give an anatomical-physiological explanation for this difference between conscious and unconscious innervations, it could be assumed that the conduction of the sensory stimuli to the motor fibres takes place in hysterical processes through subcortical centers, and not, like voluntary innervation, through the motor centers in the cortex. However, so far, knowledge of the anatomical-physiological basis of these processes is lacking, and even methods of investigating it do not exist. The psychoanalytic technique, on the other hand, makes it possible to reconstruct at least the psychic side of the psychomotor processes and to make conscious the unconscious content of them. The therapeutic significance of this procedure is that the unconscious psychic stimulus, after having become conscious, has the possibility of finding relief in the normal ways of expressing emotions which destroys the dynamic foundation of the neurotic symptoms.

Thus every emotionally conditioned disturbance

of an organic function is essentially similar to such
normal psycho-physiological processes as weeping,
laughing, or blushing. They differ from those normal
reactions, however, in three important points: 1. In the
case of a psychogenic disturbance of an organ the
emotion which seeks expression is unconscious, that
is to say, repressed. Normally the individual who
laughs or weeps is able to some degree, at least, to
define the psychological reason that impelled him to
laugh or to weep. This is not the case with patients
who are suffering from a stomach neurosis. Such
a patient is not able to describe those emotions which
are responsible for his stomach symptoms; he is not
even aware of the psychic origin of his symptoms; he
will deny it and try to find some somatic basis for his
ailment, and in so doing is, in most cases, supported
by his physician. 2. The psychogenic disturbance is an
unusual or, one should say, an incomplete expression
of a psychic tension. It does not give full relief to the
causative emotional tension in the same way as laughing or weeping do. 3. The symptom not being able
to relieve the psychic tension in the same way as
normal psychomotor reflexes do, a permanent tension
is sustained which is the cause of the chronic dysfunction.

*Critical Discussion of the Extension of the Theory
of Conversion Hysteria to the Field of
Organic Diseases*

In the writings of the pioneers of this field who first
dealt analytically with organic diseases (especially in
the writings of George Groddeck, S. Ferenczi, and
Ernst Simmel, but also in the earlier writings of Felix
Deutsch), there was a great tendency to interpret even
somatic phenomena that take place in the visceral
organs as the direct expression of a definite and
highly specific psychological content, such as an emotionally charged idea, or phantasy in the same way as
Freud has originally interpreted the psychological
significance of a hysterical paresis of an extremity or a
hysterical paresthesia. In approaching the field of organic diseases most of these authors simply applied the
theory of hysterical conversion without any modification. They overlooked the fact that Freud's view of
hysterical conversion was based on observation
of phenomena in organs which are under voluntary
nervous control and in the organs of sense-perception.
An important distinction obviously escaped their attention, namely, that in the vegetative organs the
possibility of expressing details of a psychological content is much more limited than in those organs which
are voluntarily controlled and in the organs of sense-

perception. They applied in a somewhat uncritical fashion the suggestive idea that speech is not the only function by which emotion or ideas can find a motor expression. It is unquestionably true that facial expressions and gestures come near to words in expressing even fine details of a psychic content, and that there exist also involuntary organic processes such as blushing, palpitation or diarrhoea, which are precipitated by different emotional impulses. It is obvious, however, that in contra-distinction to words, mimicry and gestures, the vegetative organs are limited in the variety of their response to psychic stimuli. The function of these organs is circumscribed and restricted to certain definite physiological accomplishments. One must consider that for the symbolic expression of ideas through speech a most complex and specifically adjusted organ is at our disposal, and it is hardly possible that any other organ can fully substitute for expressing detailed ideas which we express through those extremely complex innervations that constitute speaking. The heart can only beat, the stomach and intestinal tract have a limited variety of motor accomplishments and secretory functions, and the lungs can only perform within certain quantitative limitations and physiologically prescribed activity. To fear, as well as to sexual excitement and also to pleasurable expectations the heart will respond always with palpitation.

These general considerations alone show that the theory, which attributes to changes in visceral functions, certain specific symbolic (ideational) significance is extremely unconvincing. It is hard to believe that such a detailed psychological content as a hostile phantasy directed against a definite individual can be symbolically expressed by the functions of the stomach. To what the stomach may react is not a specific idea such as revenge against a definite person, but probably only an *emotional tonus or tendency,* which, of course, may have a very specific nature.[1]

This extension of the theory of conversion hysteria is a typical example of an error, so common in the history of science, namely, of the uncritical application to another essentially different field of concepts that have been derived from definite observations.

Another fundamental difficulty of the unmodified

[1] This type of causal interpretation of visceral disturbances, for example, the heart symbolizing the male genital, is found even in Ferenczi's writings. Also, Fenichel interprets a case of heart neurosis on the basis of the patient's identification of his heart with his super-ego! This type of causal symbolic interpretation is even then fully unjustified if the dream life of the patient contains symbolic references of a similar nature. The patient's secondary knowledge of his heart ailment may supply material ("day residue") that appears in the dream with a symbolic meaning. This, however, does not justify the assumption that such a phantasy plays a rôle in the causation of the organic symptom.

application of the theory of conversion hysteria to the disturbances of vegetative organs lies in the fact that in contra-distinction to the voluntarily controlled and sensory organs most vegetative organs have no direct psychological (certainly no ideational) representation in the mind, probably not even in the unconscious. Their relation to psychic life, particularly to ideation, is much less intimate than that of those organs in which hysterical conversion symptoms are observed: in the voluntary and sensory systems. If we had not learned of the existence of the liver from anatomy, through personal experience we would never know of it, but we have an immediate knowledge of the existence of our extremities, skin or eyes. There is no evidence whatsoever that we have even an unconscious knowledge of the existence and functioning of many of our visceral organs.

In a recent discussion Ernst Simmel emphasized the fact that in organ neuroses in contrast to conversion hysteria psychological factors are involved which belong to the earliest phases of child development (pregenital period), namely, psychological tendencies connected with nutrition and excretion.[1] This fact accounts for the important difference between conversion hysteria and organ neurosis which Simmel in his earlier writings would not recognize. As I

[1] In the Los Angeles Psychoanalytic Study Group.

have pointed out before, in this early phase the child's psychic life does not contain highly specified ideational elements, but consists mainly of general emotional trends connected with the vegetative functions.[1] The emotional sources of conversion hysteria, on the other hand, belong to later stages of development (phallic and genital phases) in which the child has already learned to speak and can verbalize his feelings, is capable of ideation and phantasy formation and becomes emotionally involved in the problems of specific human relations, of love, hate and jealousy. This fact explains why in organ neuroses only general emotional tendencies come to expression in contrast to conversion hysterias, in which the symptoms are based on specific phantasies and have a specific symbolic significance.

The greatest mistake of the previous analytical attempts to interpret psycho-somatic relations consists, however, in the fact that it was hardly ever fully taken into account that organic symptoms are usually the final result of a chain of intermediary organic processes. Deutsch, who proceeds with more methodological care than other psychoanalytic authors in this field, in an early paper clearly distinguished between initial disturbances of innervation and those morphological changes which may result following such a functional

[1] Pages 146 and 147.

disturbance of long duration.[1] As will be seen, this concept serves as a basis for our theory of the formation of peptic ulcers. But even Deutsch is not always consistent in the interpretation of organic conditions. For example, in one case he interprets pulmonary hæmorrhage as the direct expression of birth phantasies.[2] This impresses us as even more inconsistent because in the same place he considers the possibility that psychological stimuli may lead to increased adrenalin production and in turn to changes in the blood pressure. According to this latter assumption the bleeding is then not the direct expression of a phantasy but the result of a change in blood pressure, even if the whole process was initiated by a very specific psychological stimulus (specific phantasies or wishes) . To state that in such a case the end-result, the hæmorrhage, has a simple and direct relation to a specific phantasy is not very convincing. It seems unquestionable that conversion in the vegetative nervous system does not always follow exactly the same rules as in the voluntary and sensory systems in which the original concepts of hysterical conversion have been formulated. Whereas in conversion hysteria the unconscious tendency finds a direct expression in the

[1] F. Deutsch: "Biologie und Psychologie der Krankheitsgenese." *Int. Ztschr. f. Psa.* VIII: 290, 1922.
[2] F. Deutsch: "Der gesunde und der kranke Körper in psychoanalytischer Betrachtung. *Int. Ztschr. f. Psa.* XII: 498, 1926.

physical disturbances, in organic processes controlled by the vegetative nervous system often a longer chain of intermediary physiological processes is interpolated between psychological stimulus and organic end-result. It is a methodological error to attempt to interpret psychologically an organic symptom which is the end-result of an intermediary chain of organic processes, instead of trying to understand those vegetative nervous impulses in their relation to psychological factors which introduce a chain of organic events resulting in an organic disturbance.[1] Thus an ulcer of the stomach or duodenum is the direct result of a disturbance in the motor and secretory functions, which disturbance, however, may be caused by emotional factors. Yet the end-result, the ulcer, cannot be interpreted psychologically because, in itself, it has no psychological significance whatsoever. What *can* be interpreted as a direct effect of psychological factors is the hyper- or hypo-secretion and the change in the motor activity and blood supply of the stomach. Similarly even psychogenic vomiting itself may not always express anything psychological, for example, disgust, although the conditions in the stomach which

[1] See also Leon J. Saul: "A Note on the Psychogenesis of Organic Symptoms," *The Psychoanalytic Quarterly*, Vol. IV, pp. 476-483, 1935.

led to vomiting may have been called forth by psychological factors.[1]

Therefore psycho-physiological investigations must pay equal attention to psychological and physiological causal chains and carefully avoid confusion between the two series.

A Few Examples of Recent Psychoanalytic Approach to the Study and Treatment of Organic Disturbances

It is not my purpose to give even a brief review of the various etiological theories and therapeutic attempts in this field, for here we are interested only in fundamental principles.[2] I shall take for illustration only a few examples from the field of gastro-intestinal disturbances which in the last four years have been subjected to systematic analytic study in the Institute for Psychoanalysis in Chicago.[3]

A short reference will be made also to the etiology of asthma and essential hypertension, which condi-

[1] I do not question, naturally, that often a specific psychological tendency can find *direct* expression also in the vegetative system, for example, blushing, psychogenic sweating, emotionally increased peristalsis, etc.

[2] I refer the reader to a survey of the literature on psycho-somatic relationships: *Emotions and Bodily Changes*, H. Flanders Dunbar, Columbia University Press. 1935.

[3] Regarding details see "The Influence of Psychologic Factors upon Gastro-intestinal Disturbances; A Symposium," by Franz Alexander, Catherine Bacon, George W. Wilson, Harry B. Levey, Maurice Levine, *The Psychoanalytic Quarterly*, Vol. III: 501-588, 1934.

tions are being studied at the present time with the technique of psychoanalysis in the Chicago Institute for Psychoanalysis.

Although, as we have seen, the earlier theoretical views of the psychogenesis of organ neuroses have required a thorough revision, nevertheless, we could start out from valuable psychoanalytic observations. The study of the early pregenital manifestations of infantile instinctual life has led to a thorough knowledge of the child's emotional evaluation of the processes of nutrition and excretion, and has shown that these emotional attitudes persist even in the unconscious of adults. The relationship of oral-receptive and aggressive-cannibalistic tendencies to such phenomena as nausea and vomiting has been well established, as well as the relation of anal-sadistic impulses to the excremental functions and their disturbances like constipation and diarrhoea. We could also profit by previous studies of internists who have recognized for a long time the importance of psychological influences in various disorders of the gastrointestinal tract.

In our analytic studies we turned our attention at first to the manifest, emotional attitudes of patients who were suffering from the same type of gastro-intestinal disturbances. Then, in the course of analytic treatment, we have penetrated gradually layer by layer the deeper unconscious background of the overt behavior.

A. Duodenal Ulcers and Gastric Neuroses

In the formulation of our results it must be emphasized that our observations have been made on selected material of cases, in patients who manifested obvious personality problems; therefore, our etiological formulations cannot claim general validity but must be restricted to a certain type of patient.

In the cases of gastric neuroses and duodenal ulcers a common feature appeared without exception and with impressive clarity: an intensive infantile help-seeking and demanding attitude, the wish to reassume the irresponsible position of the infant, in which one is completely taken care of by the parents.

Our comparative studies on a series of cases corroborated my previous observations, which I made during the analysis of a middle-aged married man. This patient suffered for more than fifteen years from chronic gastritis and at one time even an incipient peptic ulcer was diagnosed. Operation was not undertaken, but he was treated with all kinds of dietetic and pharmacological methods without any permanent effect. I undertook an analysis, which soon revealed a strong but repressed wish to be loved and treated by his wife as an infant. The dependence of the patient's chronic stomach symptoms upon these emotions was well established through observation over many months and the connection became—as is the rule in psychoanalytic treatment—especially evident after the patient had transferred his feelings of dependence to the analyst. The analytic situation allowed him to realize dependence much more than was possible in real life in his attitude toward his wife. In this period of the "transference neurosis" the stomach symptoms disappeared, for the underlying emotion found symbolic gratification in the analytic situation. The symptoms recurred, however, when the first attempts were made to force him to see that the analysis served to gratify his infantile dependence. When this was perceived, the infantile craving was again repressed and the stomach symptoms reappeared.

In the majority of the cases this passive dependent attitude is not seen in the overt behavior; on the contrary, most of these patients exhibit on the surface an intensive ambition, and inclination for strenuous, restless activity; often they are active and successful men or women who lay particular stress on being independent in life, carrying heavy responsibilities, being obligated and in debt to no one, and accepting help from nobody. In most of the cases this surface attitude is expressed and spontaneously emphasized by the patient in the first consultation, and only in the minority of cases is the infantile receptive and demanding attitude frankly expressed.

This surface attitude of hyper-activity and ambitiousness has also been observed by different internists. Alvarez speaks of the type of efficient, active Jewish business man, the "go-getter" type, as being particularly disposed to recurrent peptic ulcers.[1] Hartman characterizes the peptic ulcer type as a man who is "encountering obstacles which prove to him trial and handicap which he must, because of his nature, endeavor to overcome." He claims that the Indians of Latin America and the Chinese coolies never have ulcers, and explains this as a result of the stoic, almost apathetic attitude, the lack of strain and ambition, characteristic of these races. According to him ulcer is a disease of the civilized world and afflicts chiefly the striving and ambitious men of Western civilization.[2]

Of necessity the internist, in observing the patient's personality, must remain at the surface. He leaves off just where the psychoanalytic work begins, which penetrates into the deeper emotional layers. As the analytic work progresses beyond this surface attitude of over-activity and ambition, the duodenal ulcer

[1] Walter C. Alvarez: *Nervous Indigestion*, Powell B. Hoeber, Inc., New York, 1931.
[2] Howard R. Hartman: "Neurogenic Factors in Peptic Ulcer," *Medical Clinics of North America* XVI, No. 6, p. 1366.

patient soon reveals his craving for infantile dependence and help. It becomes obvious that the stress upon
independence, the tendency to carry serious responsibilities, the wish for efficiency, the strenuous efforts
in life for success are only defense reactions, the result of the patient's attempt to free himself from
shame and guilty feelings that result from his extremely strong demanding and help-seeking cravings,
from his wish to reassume the irresponsible position
of the infant. This passive, help-seeking attitude reveals itself in different ways: mainly in the patient's
emotional attitude toward the analyst and in dreams.
Naturally the patient's conflict about this demanding-
receptive attitude continues to exist for a long time,
and the interviews show a very characteristic altera-
tion between help-seeking dependence and its defiant
rejection. The patient visibly wishes to indulge himself in his wish to lean on the analyst but cannot do so
without demonstrating, from time to time, his independence and emphasizing that he has no need of
any help. In these phases of the analysis many patients
suddenly refuse to assume the standard position of
the analytic sessions, to lie down on the couch; others
try to adopt a condescending, patronizing attitude
toward the analyst, only to lapse soon again into
a completely passive and receptive attitude.

One finds the same conflict situation also in patients

who suffer from gastric neuroses without any organic finding. These and other clinical observations indicate a relationship between chronic, functional disturbances of the stomach (stomach neuroses) and a certain type of peptic ulcer, the latter being the final result of the chronic, functional disturbance of long duration. While certain cases remain always functional, in others in the course of time the functional disturbance leads to ulcer formation.

Various internists have arrived at similar assumptions. Von Bergmann and Westphal assumed a causal relationship between gastric neurosis and ulcer.[1] Westphal[2] even regards the ulcer as a particularly unpleasant complication of the gastric neurosis. However, with the exception of George Draper and Grace Touraine, none of the internists went much beyond emphasizing, in general terms, the importance of neurotic personality factors. They noticed, like Alvarez and Hartman, certain manifest personality features typical for the ulcer patients. Yet not using psychiatric technique they were unable to penetrate beyond the surface and describe more precisely the psychological factors that produce the chronic dis-

[1] G. Von Bergmann: "Ulcus duodeni und vegetatives Nervensystem," *Berliner klinische Wochenschrift* 59, 1913.

[2] K. Westphal: "Untersuchungen zur Frage der Nervosen Entstehung peptischer Ulcera." *Deutsches Archiv. f. klinische Medezin* 114, 1914.

turbance of the stomach functions. George Draper and Grace Touraine, due to their finer psychological method, were able to discover beyond the manifest personality features a typical conflict situation which comes close to the above described picture.[1] They found typical of their ulcer patients a masculine protest, a rejection of unconscious female tendencies, the same tendencies which, according to our psychoanalytic study, we described as receptive-demanding impulses, which as we know are closely related to strivings commonly known as female.

We see that the psychoanalytic investigation substitutes for the previous, more general observation about the nervous component in peptic ulcer formation, a very definite statement: Intensive receptive-demanding, infantile help-seeking tendencies, if through repression or external thwarting they are excluded from gratification, maintain a permanent tension which constitutes a chronic, unconscious psychic stimulus. The comparative clinical studies have shown that the stomach functions have a specific affinity toward this type of psychic stimulus; or, in other words, repressed or thwarted receptive wishes are apt to disturb the normal functions of the stomach. The

[1] "The Man-Environment Unit and Peptic Ulcer," *Archives of Internal Medicine*, 49, 1932.

question arises now: Why should just this type of psychic tendency have a specific influence upon the functions of the stomach?

Before I try to answer this question it will be advisable to discuss briefly some clinical and experimental observations about the nervous influences in stomach disturbances. Obviously the psychic stimulus is led to the stomach through parasympathetic pathways.[1]

Harvey Cushing [2] has recently observed that in a few cases acute perforation of the stomach followed brain operations. He assumes that the physiological changes in the stomach leading to perforation are the effects of parasympathetic stimulation of the midbrain centers caused by the operation.

Richard U. Light,[3] following Cushing's suggestions, has been able to produce by pharmacological stimulation (pilocarpine) of the parasympathetic nerves, peptic ulcers. According to him the parasympathetic irritation causes local anemia of the stomach which leads to ulcer by diminishing the resistance of the stomach wall to its own product, gastric juice.

[1] Recent observations indicate the possibility of endocrine influences through the blood stream.

[2] Harvey Cushing: "The Possible Relation of the Central (Vegetative) Nervous System to Peptic Ulcers." *New England Journal of Medicine,* Vol. 205, no. 20, p. 979, 1931.

[3] Richard U. Light: "Experimental Observations on the Production of Ulcers by Pilocarpine." *New England Journal of Medicine,* Vol. 205, no. 20, p. 980, 1931.

These observations make it probable that at least some cases of gastric ulcer may have not a local but a central origin. It appears established that chronic irritation of sub-cortical centers in the brain is able to influence the local factors: the secretion of gastric juice, the motility and the blood supply of the stomach wall. Theoretically, such changes as hyper-secretion of acid or undernourishment of the stomach wall may be responsible for the development of ulcers. The stomach through local anemia is weakened in its resistance against even normal concentration of acid, or chronic hyper-acidity may afflict the stomach, even though its resistance is not specifically diminished. Although it is not yet clearly established whether the coincidence of both factors is necessary or one alone is sufficient to produce ulcer, it is sufficiently proven that both of the local factors can arise under nervous influences.

The clinical observations of Cushing and the ex-perimental observation of Light both point to the sub-cortical centers as the origin of this nervous influence.

Of course the irritation of the sub-cortical centers may have various origins. Richard Light produced parasympathetic irritation artificially by pharma-cological stimulation. In the cases observed by Cush-ing, this irritation was due to the mechanical fact of the operation. In the majority of the cases the irritation of the sub-cortical centers which through the parasympathetic pathways disturbs the stomach functions, must have some other, a more usual origin. Our analytical studies make us believe that at least in those ulcer cases which can be defined as psychogenic, the sub-cortical irritation is due to cortical, *i.e.,* psychological influences that we have described as repressed or thwarted, receptive-demanding tendencies.

We may return now to the question, why this type of infantile tendencies should have a specific disturbing influence upon the normal stomach functions.

For the trained psychoanalyst, this affinity of passive receptive tendencies to the stomach functions is not at all astonishing or unexpected. The child experiences the first gratifications of its receptive tendencies in being nourished; and thus the emotional association between the passive wish to be loved, to be taken care of, on the one hand, and the physiological functions of nutrition, on the other, is established in the very first period of postnatal development. The intuitive knowledge of this psychic connection between the wish to be loved and to be fed is reflected in the German proverb, *"Die Liebe geht durch den Magen,"* which translated into English idiom means, "The way to a man's heart is through his stomach." Indeed, the first woman, Eve, seduced Adam by giving him the apple, which is a symbolic reference to the female breasts. This symbolic reference is especially manifested in the German expression "breast apples" (Brustäpfel). Moreover, everybody knows the stereotyped situation in the love stories of the Renaissance in which the woman experienced in love introduces the love scene by an exquisite dinner and uses this time-aged and approved method of Eve to seduce an innocent youth.

If the wish to be loved by a protecting woman according to the infantile pattern is excluded from consciousness because it hurts the self-esteem of the personality, it mobilizes the emotionally associated wish to be fed. The dependence of the secretive functions and the motility of the stomach on psychic stimuli is well established through the studies of Pavlov and his school. The wish to be fed, which in such cases is independent of hunger and serves as a substitute for the repressed wish to be loved, may serve as a specific and chronic stimulus which influences the functions of the stomach.

This stimulus is independent of the normal organically conditioned stimulus, namely, the need for food and has its origin in emotional conflicts entirely independent of the physiologic state of hunger. Those individuals who because of the conflict-situation described above have to repress and abnegate their over-strong receptive cravings express them in the tacit physiologic language of the stomach functions. Such a stomach behaves all the time as if it were taking or were about to take in food. The greater the rejection of every receptive gratification in life, the greater will be this unconscious wish (we may now justifiably call it *hunger*) for receiving love and help. They want food not because of organic hunger but as a symbol of love and help.

My present notion is that the stomach under this permanent chronic stimulation behaves constantly as it does during digestion. A chronic hyper-motility and hyper-secretion may be the consequence. The empty stomach is thus constantly exposed to the same physiologic stimuli to which, under normal conditions, it is exposed only periodically when it contains or is about to receive food. The symptoms of nervous stomach, epigastric distress, heartburn and belching probably are the manifestations of this chronic stimulation which sometimes may even lead to ulcer formation.

The question as to whether a constitutional or an acquired weakness of the stomach is responsible for the fact that only certain cases of gastric neurosis develop real ulcers must be left unanswered at present.

There is much experimental and clinical evidence

for the correctness of these assumptions. Alvarez, in one of his recent studies, considers such chronic stimulation of the empty stomach as one of the etiologic factors in peptic ulcer.[1] Most interesting in this respect are the experiments of Silbermann who produced ulcers in the stomachs of dogs by sham feeding through an artificial œsophageal fistula.[2] The food which the dog swallows falls on the floor and the dog snaps it up again and goes on eating greedily for perhaps even as long as three-quarters of an hour. The result is a powerful stimulation of gastric secretion in the empty stomach which leads regularly to ulcer formation. The process at work in the patients which we have investigated can best be compared with this sham feeding of dogs. They are in a state of chronic stimulation of the stomach, not as a result of the process of nutrition, but in reaction to the psychologic stimulus of longing to be loved and to receive,

[1] Walter C. Alvarez: "Light from the Laboratory and the Clinic on the Causes of Peptic Ulcers." *American J. of Surgery*, XVIII, 1932.

"Perhaps the greatest difficulty with the patients with intractable ulcer or with a tendency to the formation of ulcers is that the gastric cells go on secreting acid at times when there is no food in the stomach to sop it up." ... p. 222.

"It might be helpful to study also the reactions of the ulcer-bearing patient to sham feeding, and more might be learned about the mechanisms which cause juice to flow when the stomach is empty." ... p. 226.

[2] I. S. Silbermann: "Experimentelle Magen-Duodenalulcuser-zeugung durch Scheinfüttern nach Pavlov." *Zentralbl. f. Chir.*, 54: 2385-2392, 1927.

or to take in aggressively what they do not get freely. Since these tendencies are repressed because of a sense of inferiority for being so receptive and because of guilt for the aggressive, "taking" wishes, they cannot find a normal outlet through the voluntary system. In seeking discharge they are converted into the wish to be fed or to eat, and this is the basis of the dysfunctions of the stomach. Of course, in addition to further psychological investigation of similar cases, further physiological corroboration of these ideas is also necessary to prove their final validity.

A very interesting corroboration of the assumption that one of the causative factors in peptic ulcer formation is the continuous secretion under the influence of chronic psychological stimuli (oral phantasies and oral tendencies) is contained in the experimental studies of Henning and Norpoth [1] in Germany and Palmer and Winkelstein [2] in America. Henning and Norpoth found a maximal permanent secretion (*maximale Dauersekretion*) of the stomach glands during the night in cases of stomach disease. The greatest number of these cases had duodenal ulcer.

[1] N. Henning and L. Norpoth: *Untersuchungen über die sekretorische Funktion des Magens während des nachtlichen Schlafes.* Archiv. f. Verdauungs-Krankheiten, *53:* 64, 1933.

[2] Asher Winkelstein: "A New Therapy of Peptic Ulcer." *American J. of the Medical Sciences, 185:* 695, 1933.

Walter L. Palmer: "Fundamental Difficulties in the Treatment of Peptic Ulcer." *Journal of the American Medical Association,* 1604-1607. 1933.

They also found high nocturnal secretion in cases of chronic gastritis and also in cases of "vegetative neurosis" with healthy stomach. Similarly Winkelstein observed high acid curves in ulcer patients produced with sham ("psychic") feeding. Furthermore, contrasted with controls, the patients with gastric or duodenal ulcer showed a high nocturnal curve of acidity. These observations are in full correspondence with our views. They show the sensitiveness of the stomach secretion of the ulcer patients to nervous stimuli and they also show that the assumed continuous secretion is present in them. It seems that not the absolute grade of hyperacidity is important but the chronic state of excitement of the stomach, the chronic secretion of gastric juice. Our studies add to these observations the actual predominance and frequency of oral tendencies and oral phantasies which we consider as those psychological stimuli which lead to the continuous secretion of gastric juice.

Finally I should like to repeat again that our whole concept regarding the psychogenic factors in peptic ulcer is based on the analytically well-established fact that the wish to be taken care of and to be helped which we have so constantly found in the investigated cases is emotionally connected in the unconscious with the wish to be fed. We do not claim originality in establishing this connection and refer to the abundant psychoanalytic literature in which this connection has been described by various authors.[1]

This explanation cannot be considered as an attempt to formulate a generally valid etiological theory of peptic ulcer. It refers to a series of observed cases, and there is no evidence whatsoever that other cases of peptic ulcer may not develop on a different and perhaps non-psychogenic basis. Moreover, our material unfortunately consists only of cases of duodenal ulcer and consequently all our conclusions are restricted to this localization of ulcers.

Finally a last question must be answered. We found in our cases of peptic ulcer and gastric neurosis a strong regression to the infantile attitude of oral receptiveness and aggressiveness. Furthermore we saw that these infantile cravings become thwarted externally by circumstances but more frequently internally by the conflict connected with the oral-receptive and oral-sadistic impulses which lead to over-compensations, to an over-emphasized independence that again in turn eliminates all legitimate normal satisfaction of the so human desire to lean on others and to be

[1] Regarding the connection of oral gratifications in the sucking period with the pleasure in taking and in being given something, I refer to the original observations of Freud and Abraham:

Freud: *Three Contributions to the Theory of Sex,* p. 43.

K. Abraham: "The Influence of Oral Erotism on Character-Formation," in *Selected Papers,* p. 399.

helped by others. We understood that this increases even more the unconscious craving for the infantile dependent rôle, which longing again mobilizes the emotionally associated wish for being fed, and that this latter wish serves as a permanent stimulus of the empty stomach and causes its dysfunction. This all seems clear and is in harmony with our psychological and physiological knowledge and explains the observed facts. However, the same intensive conflicts about oral-receptive and oral-aggressive tendencies connected with the feeling of guilt and inferiority and with the typical over-compensations are common in many forms of neurosis. The psychological situation which we have described in our peptic ulcer cases and gastric neuroses is by no means specific and restricted to these cases. Consequently the conversion of the wish to be loved and to receive into the innervations of the stomach can be considered as only one of the many possible dynamic outcomes of the same unconscious conflict-situation. Why certain individuals choose just this physiological solution remains an unanswered question which belongs to the dark, hitherto unsolved field of the "choice of neurosis." The most probable assumption is that if certain unknown organic factors coincide with the above described psychodynamic configurations, they, together with these psychic factors, will lead to ulcer formation. The constancy of the oral regression and the frequency of the over-compensation and repression of oral-receptive and oral-aggressive trends entitles us, however, to suspect this psychodynamic situation to be the outstanding psychic factor in the etiology of duodenal ulcer. The contribution of psychoanalysis to this problem ends with the description of the typical psychodynamic conditions characteristic of ulcer cases.

In the present stage of our investigations it would be too early to form a definite opinion about the therapeutic possibilities of psychoanalysis in cases of peptic ulcer. In a series of cases very favorable results have been achieved by analytic treatment, yet for definite statistical statements a much greater number of completely analyzed cases is required. Undoubtedly in all psychogenic cases only psychoanalysis can be considered as an etiological therapy, because in the long chain of events that finally lead to ulcer formation, the chronic psychic stimulus (the repressed wish to be loved, to be fed) is the first link. This causes the irritation of the sub-cortical centers which through the parasympathetic pathway produces the functional changes in the stomach itself, changes in secretion and possibly also in stomach motility and blood supply. The morphological change develops under the influence of the chronic functional disturbances (hyperacidity, etc.) and is the last link in the causal chain.

B. *Mucous Colitis*

Since we are interested now mainly in those general principles according to which psychological factors influence organic functions, we may restrict ourselves to a brief summary of the results of long and painstaking clinical investigations. The analytic study of patients suffering from chronic colitis, studies which in many cases have been continued in the Chicago Institute for Psychoanalysis for a period of one to two years, made possible the reconstruction of the content of those psychic impulses which are in causal relationship with the diarrhoea attacks of the patient. Also these patients, like the ulcer cases, show strong receptive-demanding, infantile-dependent wishes, but in contrast to the peptic ulcer patients who so frequently compensate for this infantile attitude by a surface attitude of masculinity, concentrated work and ambitious efforts in life, these patients express their activity and productivity in an extremely infantile way: through their excremental functions. The psychodynamic formula is: "I have the right to take and demand, for I always give sufficiently. I do not need to feel inferior or guilty for my desire to receive and take, because I am giving something in exchange for it." Our assumption is that the diarrhoea serves as a substitute for the giving of real values.

Apart from the psychological tendency to produce or to give, the analytic studies revealed other psychological tendencies which are causally connected with increased peristalsis and diarrhoea, namely, aggressive tendencies.

To the small child, after he acquires the feeling of disgust for the excremental act, the excrement is no longer the symbol of productivity alone, but it becomes also a tool of attack and a means of expressing hate and depreciation. (The reader is here reminded of the vulgar expressions of contempt and hate common in every language, which refer to the excremental act.) This relation of sadistic impulses to the excremental function has long been known to psychoanalysis. Regarding these psychological connections, we refer to the abundant psychoanalytic publications, especially to Jones', Brill's and Abraham's work on anal-erotism.[1]

---

[1] Regarding the gift significance of the intestinal content see Freud: "On the Transformation of Instincts with Special Reference to Anal-Erotism," in *Coll. Papers* II.

Also E. Jones: "Anal-Erotic Character Traits," in *Papers on Psycho-Analysis*, p. 691.

Regarding the relation between extravagance and neurotic diarrhoea, see especially K. Abraham: "Contributions to the Theory of the Anal Character," in *Selected Papers*, p. 387.

Regarding restitution significance of the excretory act, see Dr.

As yet we are unable to advance a detailed physiological theory to explain why and how the wish to give and produce and to attack leads to those physical changes that are responsible for the symptoms of the colitis.

It is not difficult, however, to understand why the lower end of the intestinal tract, the main function of which is elimination, is specifically suited to express activity, aggression and the wish to give. By a mechanism similar to those in the gastric cases, we assume that the peristaltic function of the intestines under the permanent psychic stimulus of the wish to eject and to give, becomes independent of the normal physiological regulations. Normally the peristaltic functions are periodically regulated by the intestinal content, but in these neurotic cases a psy-

Geza-Roheim's "Heiliges Geld in Melanesien," *Int. Ztschr. f. Psa.* IX, p. 384, 1923. In this article Roheim shows that in burial ceremonies of the Tonga Islanders the most valuable possessions of the clan are put into the grave of the dead chief but parallel with this ceremony the men evacuate their excrement on the grave.

Regarding the sadistic significance of the excretory act see K. Abraham: "The Narcissistic Evaluation of Excretory Processes in Dreams and Neurosis," in *Selected Papers.* "Returning to the sadistic significance of defecation, I may mention that the patient who killed her family in her dream by means of her excretions was severely troubled with nervous diarrhoea. Besides the usual causes, psychoanalysis discovered a sadistic element at the bottom of this symptom. Her diarrhoea proved to be an equivalent of suppressed outbursts of rage. Other analysed cases have confirmed this connection. For instance, I know a neurotic woman who reacts with diarrhoea to any event which excites anger or rage." P. 321. See also A. A. Brill: *Psychoanalysis*, p. 274-5.

chological tendency independent of the nutritional process stimulates the peristaltic functions. This explanation is based on well established findings of psychoanalysis, namely, on the unconscious emotional significance of the intestinal content as a valuable possession and gift on the one hand, and as a means of aggression on the other. The unconscious attitude which considers the intestinal content as a valuable possession and excretions as a present given to others, corresponds to the earlier coprophilic attitude of the child before it develops the negative disgust attitude toward the excreta.

Although these formulations should not be regarded as an attempt to advance a generally valid etiological theory of spastic colitis, in all of the investigated cases we were able to reconstruct a connection between the diarrhoeas and repressed unconscious tendencies of restitution or aggression. We cannot claim that all cases necessarily develop on a psychogenic basis.

In connection with our findings, an interesting question arises regarding the well-known effect of fear upon the control of the sphincters and on peristalsis. In general one can say that fear mobilizes all kinds of active-aggressive mechanisms of the individual. Cannon has shown, for example, that fear mobilizes the adrenalin production in dogs and emphasizes the teleological nature of this phenomenon in referring to the stimulating effect of adrenalin on the muscle activity and carbohydrate metabolism which the animal needs in defending itself against an external danger. He also points out other effects of the mobilized adrenalin, for example, a certain change in the distribution of blood, which is favorable in conditions of increased muscle activity.[1] It is not so easy to understand from the teleological point of view how the excremental function could ever serve for defense or attack. Psychoanalytic experience shows however that the excremental functions are deeply linked with aggressive tendencies in the emotional life, which led to the analytic concept of anal-sadism. Fear mobilizes aggression, and excremental elimination is psychologically linked up with aggression. Those who have no "guts" move their bowels under the influence of fear instead of attacking the enemy. In this perspective, the reflex mechanism of moving the bowels under the influence of fear is an example of those pathological, even if common, phenomena in which a nervous impulse is transferred from the voluntary system to the vegetative system. Instead of a muscular attack a symbolic infantile ex-

[1] W. B. Cannon: *Bodily Changes in Pain, Hunger, Fear and Rage.* Ed. 2.

pression of aggression takes place, evacuation having the symbolic meaning of attack.

Undoubtedly this interesting connection could easily lead to further speculations. The well established but peculiar connection between excremental elimination and hostile aggressiveness may be not only an infantile but an archaic mechanism. Possibly there is a fundamental psychogenic connection between active-aggressive impulses and eliminating innervations. They may belong to the same category. We see many examples in animals in which secretory and eliminating functions, squirting out offensive substances, are used for defense and aggression. The sadistic significance of the excretory act possibly follows the same psycho-physiological pattern.

The final evaluation of the therapeutic efficiency of psychoanalysis in cases of mucous colitis must also be left to the future, when a greater number of cases has been subjected to complete analysis. According to our experiences in the Chicago Institute for Psychoanalysis, the great majority of cases react most favorably to the analytic approach. Usually the patients after a relatively short period of analysis are able to give up all dietary restrictions without recurrence of their symptoms.

C. *Chronic Constipation*

An attitude characterized by pessimism and the belief that one is not loved, that one receives nothing from others, the fear of not being able to earn a living, have been found in our clinical studies characteristic of many patients suffering from chronic constipation. This character trend coincides with features described earlier by Abraham as belonging to the "anal-character." "I do not receive anything from others and therefore I do not need to give; indeed I have to cling to what I possess" is the emotional syllogism, which expresses the psychologic situation characteristic of these cases. This emotional attitude seems to be in causal connection with the tendency to retain the intestinal content. The connection lies in the unconscious evaluation of the intestinal content as valuable possessions in the coprophilic tendency of the child before and during the period of training to cleanliness. However, in these cases just as in the colitis cases, the aggressive-sadistic tendency also plays an important rôle. The patient's mistrustful, hostile attitude toward the environment, expressed in his belief that nobody loves him and nobody gives him anything of value, leads him not only to an over-possessive retentive and stingy attitude, but also to an aggressive-revengeful one. This revengeful attitude is of anal-sadistic nature. It consists in the wish to soil with excrements. The patients react to these soiling impulses with fear of retaliation and guilt, and therefore repress them. This repression of the soiling tendency leads to the inhibition of the excremental act. The result is chronic constipation.

Accordingly, chronic psychogenic constipation has a double psychodynamic background: 1. The first factor can be verbalized as follows: "I cling to my possessions; I do not wish to give away anything." 2. The excremental act is inhibited on account of its aggressive-soiling significance. The first attitude corresponds to the early coprophilic evaluation of the excremental act and the second to anal-sadistic impulses.

A short case history will give a simple illustration of these abstract formulations.

A young woman, married for two years, suffered from chronic constipation since the beginning of her marriage. Daily enemas were used. Repeated physical examinations were always negative. Before I started the analysis, the patient was observed for several days in a hospital for internal disturbances and the report was: "Organic examination negative, nervous constipation." The analysis revealed the following situation:

The young woman entered upon marriage expecting great love and tenderness. Her husband was an artist, whose chief interest was in his profession. He was entirely blind to the emotional needs of a young woman and continued a kind of bachelor existence after his marriage. The young wife had a great conscious longing for a child, but her husband refused it categorically from financial considerations and because he wanted to devote himself entirely to his art and did not want to be disturbed by increased financial and emotional responsibilities. The analysis for a long time did not give any specific clue to the symptom, although it was rather obvious that somehow it was connected with the woman's emotional reaction to her husband's behavior. In order to have my own impression of the husband and to control the objectivity of the patient's picture of her husband, I asked him to come to see me. This meeting entirely corroborated the patient's description. He gave the impression of an interesting but entirely self-centered young man who was entirely naïve and inexperienced in all female affairs. He was absolutely unable to understand my statement that his wife was basically dissatisfied with her marriage, although she herself did not want to realize this. Manifest signs of her dissatisfaction were absent, because the patient tried to deceive herself in this respect and repressed her dissatisfaction as much as was possible. She lived in the illusion of being happily married and never expressed any direct complaint against her husband.

When she said something which sounded like an accusation against him, she did it in a humorous way, as if it was a trifle not worth mentioning. To explain to the husband his lack of attention to his wife, I used an example which the patient had given me in characterizing their marital life, that since the first day of their marriage the husband never brought any small sign of attention to the house, flowers or anything else. It seems that our interview made a deep impression on the husband, and he left my office with a guilty conscience. The next day the patient reported in the analysis that she had a spontaneous bowel movement before she took her daily enema, the first time for two years. Seemingly, without any connection, she also reported in the same session that her husband for the first time in their married life had brought home a beautiful bouquet of flowers. The cathartic influence of these flowers was indeed amusing and gave us the first clue to the psychic background of the symptom. This woman had used an infantile way of expressing spite toward her husband as an answer to his loveless behavior. The psychology of early childhood knows very well this kind of infantile behavior. The small child considers the excrements as his first possession and very often uses the excremental functions to express his emotions toward the environment. During the training for cleanliness, the adults, in order to teach the child regularity, try to overcome the infantile stubbornness by promising rewards such as sweets and other gifts for correct behavior. In the vocabulary of every mother one finds the expression, "If you do it nicely, then you will get so and so." Thus the child learns very soon to consider the excrement as something which can be exchanged for other values, while its retention expresses the opposite, namely, spite and stubbornness; as if the child would say, "If you do not give me what I expect from you, I will keep it back." The constipation of the patient was an infantile reaction which she did not want to admit to herself and which she never had shown openly. She expressed in this concealed and infantile way her resentment against the loveless attitude of her husband. And indeed, the first time her husband was generous, she also became generous and gave up her obstinacy, *i.e.,* her constipation, which started a few weeks after her marriage. A further analysis revealed that upon this early infantile nucleus of spite there was superimposed another motivation, namely, the wish for getting pregnant. The constipation was also a reaction to her husband's denial to have a child. The unconscious identification of child and excrement—well known to every trained

analyst—was the basis of this reaction.[1] The consti-
pated patient surrendered in a relatively short analysis to this insight. She could not deceive herself longer
about her deep dissatisfaction with her husband's behavior, but since her resentment became conscious
there was no need to express it in this concealed and,
for an adult, unusual way. She had now to face consciously her marital problem. After the analysis was
finished, I had occasion to control the permanency
of this cure for five years, during which the constipation had not returned. The fact that a few years after
her cure she had a child probably contributed to the
permanency of this therapeutic success.

It is needless to say that not all chronic constipation is psychogenic and even all psychogenic cases
do not react so dramatically to analytic interpretations
as this one, but our therapeutic experiences in the
Chicago Institute for Psychoanalysis are most promising even in stubborn cases of constipation of long
duration.

D. *Psychological Factors in Essential Hypertension*

With the expression "essential hypertension" the
clinician refers to a group of patients suffering from

---

[1] I have in mind more an emotional than an ideational identification of excrement and child. Her wish to have a child was the
expression of her possessiveness (to possess a child) and therefore
could be gratified with the retention of excrements as a substitute.

a chronic elevation of the blood pressure, in whom the local conditions neither of the circulatory nor the adrenal system show gross deviations from the normal. Since these patients often give a tense, hyperactive and nervous impression, it is common to suspect psychic influences because it is well known that emotions like fear and rage may result in an elevation of the blood pressure.

The few cases studied in the Institute for Psychoanalysis in Chicago point to the assumption that in these cases the patient is subject to a chronic, psychic stimulus of fear and aggression of a more or less repressed nature.[1] There is much evidence that the chronic elevation of the blood pressure is a reaction to this chronic psychological condition. The psychosomatic mechanism is probably the same as in the normal reaction in which the blood pressure rises under the influence of acute emotions, the difference being only the chronic nature of the psychic stimulus. Whether or not the elevation of the blood pressure takes place under the influence of the adrenal system, which, as Cannon has shown, is under psychic control, or through direct psychological influence upon the vasomotor centers, is a problem which only physiological laboratory experiments will be able to solve.

[1] See also L. B. Hill: "Psychoanalytic Observations on Essential Hypertension," *The Psa. Review*, XXII, 1935.

E. Asthma—Urticaria—Angioneurotic Edema

Both the respiratory tract and the skin, just like the gastro-intestinal tract and the circulatory system, react normally and pathologically to psychic stimuli. Panting in fear, and sighing with relief and despair, laughter and weeping are all examples of normal respiratory reactions to psychic stimuli; blushing, on the other hand, is a skin reaction, both to shame and joy. There are also chronic, pathological conditions of both the respiratory system and the skin such as asthma, urticaria and angioneurotic edema, in which psychological factors have been suspected or assumed for a long time. These conditions often appear together in the same patient. In many cases the skin symptoms of early childhood are followed later by asthma attacks.

Both asthma and these associated skin conditions present a field of hypotheses and observations which is most controversial.

In the older medical literature it was common to speak of "asthma nervosa," and asthma was considered a neurosis, but this concept is gradually disappearing from modern medical literature. It was based on manifold observations by various clinicians that asthma attacks often are precipitated by obvious and acute emotional disturbances. Since the discovery of the phenomena of anaphylaxis and allergy, another perhaps more general factor in the causation of asthma has been described: the sensitiveness of the asthma patient to certain substances in the air and in foods. It has been satisfactorily demonstrated that attacks of asthma, edema and urticaria often occur as a reaction to the incorporation either by inhalation or through the mouth of specific irritant substances. In a large percentage (about 50%) of asthma cases, such specific sensitiveness can be demonstrated and brought in causal relationship with the asthma attacks.

The older observations about the influence of emotional factors have not been invalidated, however, by this new discovery. Careful recent observers have corroborated the older statements that asthma attacks both in sensitive (allergic) and non-sensitive patients often take place under the influence of emotional factors.[1]

The rôle of emotional factors in asthma and certain skin conditions constitutes the main topic of our research activities at present in the Institute for Psy-

[1] See literature in H. Flanders Dunbar, *Emotions and Bodily Changes,* Col. Univ. Press, New York, 1935; and in particular Eduardo Weiss, "Psychonalyse eines Falles von nervösen Asthma," *Internationale Zeitschrift für Psychoanalyse,* Vol. VIII, No. 4, 1922, pp. 440-455.

choanalysis in Chicago. It is too early to attempt any general formulations in this field.

A General Etiological Scheme of Psychogenic Organ Disturbances

The combination of clinical, physiological and psychoanalytic approaches in the study of peptic ulcer formation gives us an etiological formula which can be considered as a general pattern of many organ neuroses and psychogenic organic diseases. In the long chain of causative factors the following links can be distinguished:

1. Chronic psychic (cortical) stimulus (repressed tendency.
2. Excitation of sub-cortical centers through psychic stimulation.
3. Conduction of the excitation of the sub-cortical centers to different vegetative organs through the vegetative nervous system (parasympathetic and sympathetic pathways) producing local changes in the vegetative functions.
4. Morphological tissue changes under the influence of the chronic functional disturbance.

In cases which do not progress to the last link (4) we speak of *organ neurosis* or of a functional disturbance; in cases in which the pathological processes progress as far as the end phase (4), that is to say, in cases in which eventually permanent structural changes in the tissues appear, we speak of an *organic disease*. This etiological scheme follows up in continuity the pathological process step by step through its different phases and eliminates all the obscurity and mystery about psychologically conditioned organic processes. The rough morphological changes in the tissues are not direct effects of psychological forces but are conditioned by a chronic, probably quantitative disturbance of the physiological function of the organ. That such a functional disturbance may have a central (psychological) origin is common knowledge; psychoanalysis adds to this knowledge the precise description of the psychological factors.

According to this view the difference between organ neurosis and conversion hysteria lies mainly in the localization of the symptoms and in the difference of the pathways through which the original psychological tension (stimulus) finds its somatic expression. In conversion hysteria the psychological tension finds direct expression in voluntarily controlled organs and in the organs of sense-perception, *i.e.*, in organs, which execute the interaction of individual and environment, and which consequently are in permanent contact with mental life in general and with ideation in special. In organ neuroses the emotional tension influences via the vegetative nervous system the function of vegetative organs, which have

no direct relation to ideation. This may explain why
in organ neuroses the symptoms do not express
specific ideational content, as, for example, phantasies
as they do in conversion hysteria, but only general
emotional trends. Common, however, for both disturbances—for conversion hysteria and organ neuroses
—is the fact that they are the last results of the
patient's disturbed emotional relation to his environment. They are unconsciously conditioned innervations, and are substitutes for voluntary actions, which
the patient cannot carry out because their motivation
is rejected by the conscious ego and consequently
repressed. In the organ neuroses, however, also the
division of labor between the functions of the cerebro-
spinal and the vegetative nervous system is disturbed.
As has been already discussed in Chapter V,[1] the
structure of the nervous system manifests a certain
division of labor in that the relation to the environment, on the one hand, and the regulation of the
inner processes, on the other hand, are divided between the cerebro-spinal and the vegetative nervous
system. The voluntary innervations, which are subject to the control of the cerebro-spinal system, regu-
late the attitude to the environment; the inner
vegetative processes are controlled by the automatic
functions of the vegetative centers. An organ neurosis

[1] Pages 162 to 164.

represents a confusion in the division of labor of the
nervous system: the dividing line between the inner
and foreign politics of the organism is mixed up. If
a psychodynamic quantity which under normal conditions would lead to an external action becomes
repressed, it takes a wrong pathway and instead of a
voluntary or genital innervation it leads to innervations in the vegetative systems. Thus, for example, in
the place of the normal expression of love or hate,
an inner process is influenced. This pathological
deviation of a psychodynamic quantity from external
action, that is to say, from voluntary innervation to
the innervation of a vegetative organ, can be compared with a social phenomenon, which so often takes
place in the politics of the nations. Ambitions in the
field of foreign politics which become frustrated by a
military defeat usually lead to an overheated atmosphere in the inner politics of the nation. This is best
shown by the fact that revolutions start usually after
lost wars and that the method which has proved to be
the best to check revolutionary movements is to start
military action against a foreign nation. Inner social
tensions can be best relieved by diverting the energies
that are engaged in inner affairs outward in conduct-
ing them into the channels of foreign politics. And,
vice versa, the decrease of the possibilities of active

foreign politics enhances the danger of inner social difficulties.

Every neurosis, no matter whether it is expressed merely by psychic processes or by bodily disturbances of functional nature, is the result of a defeat of the individual in his psychic relation to the environment, in his foreign politics. Every hysterical organ disturbance is the dynamic substitute for omitted actions. In organ neuroses, however, the emotions and wishes to which the individual cannot give expression and relief in social or sexual activities find expression in the unintelligible tacit language of inner vegetative processes.

Vector Analysis of Psychological and Biological Forces

It has been pointed out before that in studying the influence of psychological factors upon vegetative functions, in the first place the patient's general emotional attitudes and the dynamic direction of his impulses must be considered rather than the specific ideational content of the psychological material.

These general attitudes can be described in dynamic terms expressing, as it were, the direction of the patient's major tendencies. We could differentiate three major dynamic directions or "vectors," characteristic of emotional tendencies—the wish to incorporate (to take in), to eliminate, and to retain. These are abstractions which correspond, however, to very well-defined emotional attitudes. The vector tendency to *incorporate* is common in many different psychological attitudes, such as the wish to receive a gift, the wish for a child, or love, attention, to be fed, or to take away something from another person. Similarly many attitudes possess the common quality of *elimination;* to give in a constructive way, for example, a gift, love, attention, to make an effort for the sake of another, to create something of value; and also destructively by attacking or soiling another person, especially by throwing something at him. The wish to *retain* is also a common characteristic of many different psychological attitudes in which holding on to a possession is the major vector quality.

During the analysis of organ neuroses we observed that very different psychological impulses with quite different specific content may lead to the disturbance of the same organic function provided that they possess the same vector quality: incorporation or elimination or retention. At first sight it seems that the different psychogenic factors which are apt to influence the same organic functions are not at all specific, or in other words, that the same disturbance can be caused by a great variety of psychological contents, seemingly unrelated to each other. Further analysis of these apparently unrelated psychic factors showed, however, that they had one important feature in common, *i.e.,* the direction of the general dynamic tendency which we call their *vector* quality. So, for example, organs which have the function of incorporation such as the stomach or the lungs in their inspiratory activity are apt to be disturbed by very different repressed tendencies. These tendencies, however, have one dynamic feature in common, *i.e.,* they all express receiving or taking something *(incorporation)*. It has been observed that this general dynamic direction of a psychological content is related to the kind of organ function which will be disturbed by it. The stomach functions can be disturbed, for example, by any one of the following heterogeneous group of repressed wishes: the wish to receive help, love, money, a gift, or the wish for a child; or the wish to castrate, to steal, to take away something. The same group of wishes may also disturb other organic functions which involve incorporation, for example, the inspiratory phase of the respiratory act, or swallowing. The common feature in all these different tendencies is their centripetal direction: they express receiving or taking something. Thus our first category is *incorporation*.

Also the second dynamic category, that of *elimination* tendencies, includes an enormous variety of psychological contents: on the one hand, to give love, to make an effort, to help to produce something, to give a gift, to give birth to a child; on the other hand, the wish to attack someone (especially by throwing something at him). Any of these impulses, if repressed and excluded from voluntary expression, are apt to influence eliminating organic functions such as urination, defecation, ejaculation, perspiration, or the expiratory phase of respiration.

The third dynamic quality, the significance of which became apparent during the analysis of gastrointestinal neuroses, that of *retention*, again includes a great variety of different psychological contents. These all share the one common dynamic quality—that of retaining or possessing. For example, collecting different objects, putting them in order and classifying them (as a sign of the mastery of them), also the fear of losing something, the rejection of the obligation to give something, the impulse to hide things to prevent their being taken away or to protect them from deterioration, and the mother's protective attitude toward the foetus—all these frequently find expression in retentive physiological innervations. The best known of these is constipation, but it seems also that the retention of urine, retarded ejaculation, and certain features of the respiratory act, can express the same tendencies.

Thus we differentiate three large categories of psychological tendencies representing the three vector qualities: *incorporation, elimination* and *retention.* During our studies we have learned that for the purpose of psychological understanding it is necessary to differentiate further in each of these categories between a positive or constructive, and a negative or destructive manifestation of the same tendency. In the first group, the incorporating tendencies, we differentiate between a tendency to receive passively and to take away aggressively. In the second group, the eliminating tendencies, we again distinguish between the wish to give or produce something of value from an aggressive attacking form of elimination (for example, anal soiling tendencies). And finally in the group of retentive tendencies we separate the wish to retain something in order to use the material retained for the constructive purpose of "building up" (as in growth) from the destructive wish of withholding something of value from others as a sign of hostility. It is evident that the three main categories of vectors express fundamental urges, whereas the six subclasses are more complex tendencies which express not only the direction of the tendency but also a certain attitude (love or hate) toward external objects. It must be emphasized, however, that regarding its dynamic effect upon different vegetative functions the main vector quality, the incorporating, eliminating or retentive nature of a psychological tendency, determines what type of organic function will be disturbed by it.

VECTOR ANALYSIS OF PSYCHIC TENDENCIES

Tendencies classified according to their Fundamental Dynamic Quality (Direction).	*Tendencies in Relation to Objects.*
Incorporation. . . .	To receive To take
Elimination	To give a value or produce something of value To eliminate in order to attack
Retention	To retain in order to build up [1] To withhold from others

This analysis of psychological impulses according to their vector qualities is therefore of great value for the understanding of psycho-somatic interrelationships, because the vector qualities express .psychological tendencies and at the same time also correspond to the major vegetative functions of the organism: the *incorporation* of energy and substances, their *retention* in the process of growth, and their *elimination* in the form of waste products, procreation, and mechanical energy and heat.

---

[1] This tendency does not express an object relation, but a relation to the self as an object.

It seems to us that in the concept of psychological and biological vectors we have found the common denominator of psychological and biological processes. The organism can indeed be considered a mechanism the fundamental functioning of which (metabolism) can be well understood and described in the terms of the three vectors of incorporation, retention and elimination. The analysis of the psychological attitudes leads us to elementary tendencies that can be described in terms of the same vectors. Thus the assumption seems to be justified that these psychological tendencies or vectors are nothing but the subjective perception on the part of the organism of its fundamental biological processes; or, in other words, the psychological dynamics is the subjective reflection of the biological dynamics of life.

The same point of view is applicable not only to the function of the whole organism, but also to the function of many specific organ systems, for example, the gastro-intestinal tract with its three-fold function of incorporation, elimination and absorption (retention); or to the three-fold function of the lungs which consists also of an inspiratory (incorporating) and expiratory (eliminating) function, and the absorption of oxygen as a retentive function.

As yet the vector analysis has proven its usefulness mainly in the study of those organ systems which have an opening on the body surface and whose function consists in an exchange of substances with the environment and whose physiological activity consists in incorporation, elimination and retention (the gastro-intestinal tract, respiratory system, genito-urinary system, and to a certain degree, the skin). The psychologically conditioned disturbances in the function of these organs (organ neuroses) can be understood as the result of a disturbed emotional balance between incorporating, eliminating and retaining tendencies. These tendencies or vector qualities determine the type of vegetative organ functions which will be disturbed by them in the case of an organ neurosis.

Such a disturbance of the emotional balance takes place if these major attitudes or tendencies cannot, because of psychoneurotic conflicts, find a normal expression in the individual's social and sexual relationship.[1]

Conclusions

The purpose of this writing is not to give a full account of all the usual and possible psycho-physiological interrelations, but to show in general outlines how psychoanalytic research is able to give a specific,

[1] The general theory of such organ neuroses in the light of vector analysis is discussed more fully in my article "The Logic of Emotions and Its Dynamic Background," *The International Journal of Psychoanalysis*, Vol. XVI, Part 4, October, 1935.

empirically founded content to the vague concept of "functional disturbances with psychic origin." [1] At present, modern medicine is more inclined to take into account psychic stimuli and even to recognize their omnipresence and fundamental importance for certain functional disturbances, but the concept of the psychic stimulus remains an empty generality if its intimate nature is unknown. In the general form, however, the modern physician is more inclined to accept the psychic causation of some symptoms, but shows resistance and skepticism if the psychoanalyst tells him about specific wishes, striving, fears, etc., which are the primary cause of so many functional and even organic diseases.[2] The only way, however, to

[1] Cf. William A. White: "Medical Psychology," p. 132. *Nervous and Mental Diseases Monograph Series* No. 54, New York, 1931. "The fact that there is a psychological factor in connection with all disease seems to be inevitable if the theory of what constitutes psychological reaction developed in this book is accepted. The specificity of the reaction, however, is the particular thing that now calls for explanation and elucidation. That there is such a specific correlation seems inevitable but to define it undoubtedly presents one of the most difficult problems of medicine."

[2] This increasing interest of physiologists in psychic factors is best reflected in the experimental studies of W. B. Cannon on the influence of emotions upon organic processes. (W. B. Cannon: *Bodily Changes in Pain, Hunger, Fear and Rage*, page 264, 2nd edit. D. Appleton and Company, New York, 1929.) But even in this excellent study the discrepancy between the specificity of the physiological data described and the generality of psychological facts and ideas is very obvious. The author's apparent unfamiliarity with the details of psychic, especially unconscious, phenomena becomes most manifest in his discussion of clinical cases and therapy. "... the *occasion* for worries, anxieties, conflicts, hatreds, resent-

prove the statement of psychoanalysts is to look into the psychological microscope, *i.e.,* to undertake the long and painstaking investigation of patients according to the prescriptions of the psychoanalytic technique. Philosophical arguments, that a wish to be loved by one's own wife in an infantile way cannot possibly produce indigestion and stomach pains, which are based on physicochemical processes, are futile and unscientific. The unusual nature of a phenomenon is no proof against its existence, and because we do not know the detailed mechanism of a causal connection between two facts does not justify its denial. The fact that longing to be loved like an infant occasionally produces stomach symptoms or repressed spite may cause constipation is no more mystical than laughter, *i.e.,* the convulsive contraction of the diaphragm and laryngeal muscles as a result of seeing a comic situation or hearing a good anecdote.

In many cases even of organic diseases, a complete case history which claims to give a full etiological explanation has to contain besides the usual somatic

ments, and other forms of fear and anger, which affect the thalamic centers, must be removed. In short, the factors in the whole situation which are the source of strong feeling must be discovered and either explained away or eliminated" (p. 264). In this remark the over-simplification and the lack of any reference to the real therapeutic problems, with which the elaborate technique of psychoanalysis has to cope, show that the author is either not informed of the results of modern psychotherapy or does not want to give credit to them.

data gained in the medical laboratories details of facts regarding the development of the patient's personality and his psychological situation. Only these data can give us an account of those specific repressed tendencies, which in time may lead to tangible morphological changes in the organs, although for a long time they may have caused merely functional disturbances. The etiological formula of many organic disturbances follows this scheme: chronic psychic stimulus (repressed tendency)—functional disturbance—organic (morphological) changes.

The desire that in the future the knowledge of psychological factors should be replaced by the knowledge of the corresponding physiological processes of the brain is a respectable one, but so long as it is only a desire it is no substitute for the actual knowledge of the relation between psychic facts and physiological processes. The abundant hypothetical assumptions about unknown cellular processes in the brain, which a German physiologist appropriately has called "brain mythology," cannot replace well-known psychic facts. Preferring such histological phantasies to psychological facts is like substituting hopes for the future for exact observations which we have in the present. Moreover, it is a great question whether even an accurate notion of the cortical processes which accompany psychological phenomena will ever be able to account for the complicated relations of the individual to his environment as clearly as psychological understanding. I think, therefore, that even when we possess the knowledge of the complete physiological causality of biological processes, we shall not be willing to dispense with psychological insight into the functioning of the mental apparatus.

VII.

Psychoanalysis in Medical Education

THE reader should now understand why psychoanalysis has had to become so awkward a problem in medicine. In the long run, it is an impossible situation that a theory which furnishes a better understanding of many diseases than has been previously possible and a therapy which is not only able to cure symptoms, but to give a scientific account of their origin and nature, should be entirely disregarded. If it is true that ailments like certain forms of chronic gastritis and constipation or functional heart trouble can be better understood and cured with greater success than with previous methods, then psychoanalysis must become an integral part of medicine and must become part of the physician's education. The only way to avoid this conclusion is either to deny the achievements of psychoanalysis, or, what is more usual, to refuse to take notice of it.

Any other course necessitates a radical change in medical education and involves either admitting that the medical student should know the structure and functioning of the personality as well as anatomy and physiology, or acknowledging the psychological approach to organic disturbances as valuable but distinct. This attitude would preserve the homogeneous physico-chemical basis of modern medicine without doing injustice to psychoanalysis. If such a division of the somatic and psychological approaches were admitted, medical therapy and psychotherapy would become two different professions and the physician could save his field from an invasion by psychology. It is, however, evident that even if such a division were practicable, the physician ought to know the fundamentals of psychoanalysis and the psychotherapists the principles of general pathology.

Freud inclines to the second solution in his book on "Lay-Analysis," but I feel that no argument can be entirely convincing with the little experience we have to go on. There are no doubt good psychotherapists who have had no thorough medical training and background and good physicians who are unacquainted with psychoanalysis, but "good" is a relative word, and the possibility of increasing the efficiency of the psychotherapists with medical knowledge and that of the physician by analytic training should not be neglected. I have become recently more and more convinced that the separation of the psychological and somatic approaches is artificial, out-of-date, and contradicts the philosophical postulate that biological systems are psycho-biological entities. This postulate, however, agrees best with our present knowledge of biological systems. I would consider it tactless to guess at Freud's subjective reasons for wishing his own creation to remain separate from medicine if his motives did not have so profoundly human a justification. There is no question that Freud deeply resents the refusal of medicine to appreciate his life work. The laughter with which the young Freud was received in the medical association in Vienna, when he returned from Paris and reported his new experiences with Charcot, will remain always a classical example of the dogmatic attitude of medicine toward its great representatives, and reminds one of the reception of Harvey's, Pasteur's and Semmelweis' discoveries by their contemporaries. Freud's resentment toward academic medicine is a reflection of his own bitter experience. Science, however, is impersonal and its development is independent of the fate of individuals. Medicine cannot avoid adopting psychoanalytic theory and methods and his followers must hope that Freud may witness the practical coöperation of psychoanalysis and medicine.

The experiment at the University of Chicago of introducing a psychoanalyst into the medical faculty will be followed by others, and their success will grow with the increasing desire of the medical profession to be informed of the details of psychoanalytic research.

There are, however, certain practical difficulties in the way. As long as teaching and research in psychoanalysis remain the private affair of a relatively small group of trained psychoanalysts, difficulty will be experienced in organization of education and in the making of detailed reports and special studies.

A few practical suggestions on the inclusion of psychoanalytic training in medical schools may now be added.

In introducing a new discipline, we do not have to cope with traditional habits and can, therefore, follow a purely logical and systematic plan. Training in psychoanalysis has been carried on in the past outside the medical schools and universities—in the Psychoanalytic Institute.[1] The students of these Institutes are for the most part medical students and physicians, especially psychiatrists, social workers, students of education, and in recent years lawyers, especially criminologists. An intelligent combination of their

[1] The first Psychoanalytic Institute was founded by Dr. Max Eitingon in Berlin in 1920. In the course of ten years he has developed it into a real Academy of Psychoanalysis and all the younger Institutes have adopted his principles of organization.

original studies with psychoanalytic training was, however, impossible, since the Psychoanalytic Institutes had no official connection with recognized academic schools. These Institutes live an isolated existence, which has had the single advantage that they have been undisturbed by external interference and could teach their own principles without compromise. The isolation of the Psychoanalytic Institutes arises not only from historical circumstances, but from the nature of psychoanalysis itself.

As a psychological theory, psychoanalysis became relevant to all disciplines dealing with the human mind. It occupies a central position in psychological science similar to that of chemistry in the natural sciences. Chemistry is needed in medicine, in technology, in agriculture, but no one would consider chemistry as a part of medicine, agriculture, or technology. Similarly, a knowledge of the psychological structure and functions of the mind is just as important for anthropology, sociology, criminology, esthetics, philology, and history as for the understanding and treatment of mental diseases. Therefore psychoanalysis cannot be considered a part of medicine or psychiatry, because of its more general nature. Psychoanalytic Institutes as scientific and educational units will not be superfluous even if psychoanalysis becomes a part of regular medical training.

A knowledge of the development and functions of the mind became important for psychiatry once it was empirically established that most mental disturbances, apart from constitutional factors, are determined by the psychological experiences of postnatal development. The detailed study of the influences affecting the development of the personality by highly refined and specifically adjusted methods of investigation is almost exclusively the accomplishment of Freud and his school.

A recent and extremely valuable addition, however, to this field has been made, chiefly under the influence of William Healy. This contribution of American psychiatry, appropriately called "social psychiatry," has developed a new instrument in psychiatric research, the psychiatric social worker, whose work rapidly developed into a new profession. The social worker investigates the patient's environment and furnishes the psychiatrist with "objective" data about the patient's actual life, which can be compared with the "subjective" data received from the patient himself. Healy and I have used this technique in our study of criminal individuals.[1]

But let us return to the problem of the psychoanalytic training of the medical student. There is no bet-

---

[1] F. Alexander and W. Healy, *Roots of Crime*, Knopf, New York, 1935.

ter proof of the psychiatrist's need for psychoanalytic training than the noteworthy fact that in Europe, as well as in this country, a considerable part of the rising generation of psychiatrists regard the study in one of the Psychoanalytic Institutes as a necessary complement to their training. During their studies of psychoanalysis they come, without exception, to the conclusion that the new psychodynamic point of view is more helpful in the understanding and handling of psychoneurotics and psychotics than anything they learned during their regular university training. The paradoxical situation arises that young psychiatrists receive their most important training outside the medical schools.

The same situation is reflected in current psychiatric literature. The basic concepts of the Freudian doctrine have penetrated and reformed modern psychiatric thinking. Since I have already referred to this fact, a brief repetition may suffice. The understanding of paranoid phenomena as the projection on to others of unacceptable tendencies, the estimate of schizophrenic behavior patterns as regressions to infantile forms of thinking and feeling, the recognition of psychoneurotic symptoms as dynamic results of repression, the understanding of melancholic self-accusation, self-depreciation, and suicide as introverted aggressions, are generally accepted as the best causal explanation of these disturbances. In so far as psychiatry has progressed from the mere macroscopic description of psychological features in mental diseases in the Kraepelinian sense and has become an explanatory science, it is based on Freudian views. Moreover, it is a matter of common observation that textbooks of psychiatry which are either ambivalent or hostile to psychoanalysis use Freudian concepts, with slight changes in terminology, whenever they attempt to explain psychological connections. In fact, in psychiatry, it is necessary only to discard the label to drink the otherwise forbidden Freudian draught.

It is not necessary to repeat the reasons why the young psychiatrist has to learn modern psychopathology outside the universities in private institutions and frequently at a financial sacrifice. Denied support, education in psychoanalysis is at present a private undertaking. This circumstance alone is responsible for the unusual expense which training in psychoanalysis involves.[1]

The importance of psychoanalysis for psychiatry should be sufficient to warn the medical authorities that it must not be left to the private initiative of the students to learn the basic concepts of psychopathology

[1] Recently The Chicago Institute for Psychoanalysis received generous support from the Rockefeller Foundation. This made possible a substantial reduction in the expenses of training in this Institute.

which in the last two decades have proved therapeutically more useful and productive than the morphological investigation of the central nervous system. There is no justification for assuming that this condition will last. Progress in science has always followed advance in methodology and although the prevailing methods of brain research seem to be approaching their limit, no one can tell when new inventions will enlarge the possibilities of somatic research.

Teaching, however, cannot be based upon future possibilities. For the understanding and handling of the neurotic and insane, the knowledge of psychopathology which is at present based on the dynamic psychology of Freud and his school is of decisive importance. In training the psychiatrist, the acquaintance with psychoanalysis has proved to be at least as important as somatic studies. There is no objective justification for the one-sided and primarily somatic training of the psychiatrist. Teaching and research cannot for long be guided by the specialized interest of individual scientists and by their apprehension lest this new and unfamiliar approach might detract from their importance and endanger their exclusive control of the field.

The special training of the psychiatrist should be divided in two equal parts: Training in the morphology and physiology of the central nervous system and its disturbances and in psychoanalytic normal psychology and psychopathology.

The inclusion of psychoanalysis in the special training of psychiatrists requires very little formal change in present education, since some kind of medical psychology is usually a part of any psychiatric course, although in many medical schools every kind of psychology is either banned even from psychiatric lectures, or reduced to a negligible quantity. The fundamental importance of psychogenic factors in "organ neurosis," *i.e.,* the functional disturbances of the inner organs, makes it necessary, however, that a course in psychoanalytical normal psychology should be placed at the beginning of the medical curriculum, parallel with the course in normal anatomy and physiology. This course should prepare the student for the understanding of functional disturbances in his later courses in internal medicine. I gave a similar course in the University of Chicago and the terminal examination corroborated my expectation that the introduction to general psychodynamic concepts can be successfully given at the very beginning of the medical curriculum. This course should contain the empirical observations most important for the understanding of unconscious mental processes, *i.e.,* the different manifestations of unconscious motivation in overt behavior. I refer in the first place to the following phenomena: hypnotism and post-hypnotic experiments, the errors of everyday life, the psychology of day-dreaming and dreams. Furthermore, this course should give a general presentation of mental development, especially of instinctual life.

The major part of psychoanalytic study, however, could best be given during the training in clinical psychiatry, but before deciding on the most advantageous schedule a few preliminary considerations should be discussed. In giving my own experience, I must say that my only regret has been that in the first period of my psychiatric work in the University Hospital in Budapest I had to deal with psychotics without the knowledge of Freud's work. In comparing this period with the following when I had taught myself some psychoanalytic theory, I can only describe the difference by comparing the situation of a tourist who is travelling in a foreign country with a knowledge of the language and customs of the inhabitants with that of another who lacks this knowledge. Once in possession of the code to the unconscious, the confusing variety of psychotic manifestations became intelligible human manifestations which could be treated intelligently.

Although the advantages of a preliminary knowledge of psychoanalysis in clinical work are evident, the general experience of the last ten years has led to

the unanimous conclusion that a thorough understanding of the unconscious processes is only possible
through didactic analysis. I cannot here justify in detail the requirement of the International Psychoanalytic Association that study of psychoanalysis should
follow the didactic analysis, and must refer to a recent
publication *"Zehn Jahre Berliner Psychoanalytisches
Instituts,"* edited by the Berlin Psychoanalytic Institute.

The necessity for the didactic analysis of the psychiatrist makes it difficult for clinical study in general
psychiatry to follow the factual psychoanalytic training. The best arrangement seems to be that the didactic analysis should take place simultaneously with or
immediately following interneship in a psychiatric
hospital, and we must content ourselves by preparing
the student for his hospital work with a general presentation of the principles of psychodynamics at the
beginning of his curriculum, and by a course in general psychiatry during the clinical semesters. This
course would correspond to the usual descriptive presentation of psychiatry, but given from the psychoanalytic point of view. During or immediately following
the interneship, which should last at least two years,
the detailed study of the psychoanalytic theory of neuroses and psychoses and of the psychoanalytic technique should be made.

First—the Berlin Psychoanalytic Institute has worked out a schedule based on ten years' experience. This scheme with some modifications has been accepted by all Institutes for Psychoanalysis, and in its present form can be considered as the most satisfactory curriculum.

This curriculum consists of three consecutive sections:

1. The student's own didactic analysis.
2. The theoretical training.
3. Practical training in the form of controlled analyses and participation in technical colloquium.

This third portion of the training needs some further explanation.

A controlled analysis means weekly consultation with a trained analyst. During this consultation a detailed report of the course of treatment conducted by the student is given and technical questions are discussed. A similar procedure is carried out in the technical colloquium in which several students participate. Since public demonstrations of technique, as in surgery, are impossible, these seem to be the only possible forms of practical training.

Section 2 (theoretical training) is devoted to courses on medical psychoanalysis but contains also a notable feature in courses of a more sociological and humanis-

PLAN OF STUDY FOR A COMPLETE PRACTICAL TRAINING IN PSYCHOANALYSIS
(Established in the Berlin Institute for Psychoanalysis)

I. *Instruction-analysis* (Didactic-Analysis)
II. *Theoretical Training* (Prescribed Courses)

	First Year	Second Year
Fall Trimester (October-December)	1. Introduction to Psychoanalysis, Part I. (Analytic Normal Psychology.) 2. Introduction to interpretation of dreams. 3. Freud seminar: Three contributions to sexual theory.	1. Special theory of the neuroses, Part II. (Character disturbances, addictions, perversions, narcissistic neuroses, psychoses, criminality.) 2. Psychoanalytic technique, Part I. 3. Freud seminar: theoretical writings, Part I.
Winter Trimester (January-March)	1. Introduction to psychoanalysis, Part II. (General theory of the neuroses.) 2. Theory of instincts. 3. Freud seminar: Case histories, Part I.	1. Psychoanalytic technique, Part II (including indications). 2. Psychoanalysis and Sociology. 3. Freud seminar: theoretical writings, Part II.
Spring Trimester	1. Special theory of the neuroses, Part I. (Transference neuroses.) 2. Application of psychoanalysis to Literature and Art. 3. Freud seminar: Case histories, Part II.	1. Psychoanalysis and Education. 2. Symbolism and art of interpretation. 3. Freud seminar: Writings on Technique.

III. *Further Training*

1. Practical Studies in Therapy (Controlled Analyses)
2. Technical Colloquium.

tic character that deal with the application of psycho-analysis to art and literature and sociology. In introducing these latter courses, we have proceeded from the experience that candidates who have some acquaintance with the humanities are far superior in their psychological understanding of the mentally sick to candidates trained only in medical and natural science. Next to the dream, the clearest manifestations of the unconscious are found in art and literature, especially in the popular art, customs, and superstitions of primitive peoples. Furthermore, sympathy with the emotional life of others is more characteristic of the man of philosophic and literary culture than one who, though medically trained, knows nothing of the emotional life of the sick or of psychology in general.

To sum up my proposition: the teaching of psycho-analysis in medical schools should take place in three different required courses, the first two for undergraduates and the last one for graduates:

1. Elementary introduction in Psychoanalytical Normal Psychology, ([a] Manifestations of the Unconscious, [b] Development of the Personality) given at the beginning of the medical curriculum parallel with the courses in anatomy and physiology.

2. Theoretical course in general psychiatry, one

part of which should be devoted to psychoanalytical psychopathology.

3. Training in psychoanalysis during or following the interneship in a psychiatric hospital consisting of (a) didactic analysis, (b) theoretical training and (c) practical training.

The third part of this scheme is well established through many years' experience at the Psychoanalytic Institutes and has actually been followed by many young psychiatrists of both continents. Its introduction into the official post-graduate training of psychiatrists does not involve any innovation or experimentation and would mean merely the official and formal sanction on the part of the medical faculties of a procedure which is followed more and more by the younger psychiatric generation.

The first two suggestions about the teaching of psychoanalysis during the undergraduate medical curriculum, however, involve a fundamental innovation. The significance of this innovation would be that the medical school would accept the view that the human system is not merely biological, but psycho-biological, and that training in medicine should consequently be based on a knowledge of the personality as well as of the body.

If I have succeeded in convincing the medical profession that the present state of affairs, in which a fundamental, practical and theoretical contribution to medicine is excluded from the medical schools, is unjustified and undesirable, this book will have served its purpose.

INDEX

HALLUCINATION, 104, 116
in the psychotic, 116, 118
paranoid, 119 f.
Harrison, William T., 16
Hartman, Howard R., 202, 204
Harvey, 250
Healy, William, 253
Heart, peripheral ganglia of,
167
psychogenic disturbance of, 56,
168, 248
Henning, N., 212
Hill, L. B., 229
Hinsie, L. E., 113 f.
Histology, 40
Hospital, psychiatric, 112, 258
Bloomingdale, 112
Budapest, 258
Menninger Clinic, 112
the McLean, 112
the Shepherd and Enoch
Pratt, 112
Hydrophobia, 60
Hyper-acidity, 207, 217
Hypertension,
essential, 228
and fear and aggression, 229
etiology of, 133, 198
study of, at Institute for
Psychoanalysis in Chicago, 199,
229
Hypnoid state, 61
Hypnosis, 53-62
abreaction of emotions in, 20,
54, 58, 61, 64 f.
as a legitimate method of
research, 159
"cathartic," 20, 57
elimination of consciousness
in, 63 f.
experiments in, 59
limitations of, 59, 62, 65
practised by Charcot, 159
recollection in, 53, 57
treatment by, 59

Hysteria,
conversion hysteria and
organic disease, 188 f.
conversion hysteria, theory of,
191
cure of, 57
dysfunctions in, 27
extension of theory of
conversion hysteria to the field
of organic diseases, 191-198
hysterical innervations, 56
symptoms of, 56 f.
symptoms of, experimentally
reproduced, 159

ID, 22, 25, 80 ff., 91
Identification, 36, 43
narcissistic, in schizophrenia,
126
of patient with persons with
whom he has continuous
contact, 126
possibility of, 37
with parents, 76
Illusion, in the psychotic, 116,
118
Incest, 78
Infant, mental life of, 38
mental processes of, 21
Infantile sexuality, 29, 67-70
prejudice against, 68
Inferiority, sense of, 73
Innervation, autonomic and
central, 168
difference between conscious
and unconscious, 189
hysterical, 55 f.
in relation to the
environment, 234
motor, 55, 84, 87, 160 f., 161,
168
voluntary, 160 f., 188 ff., 235
voluntary, and the conscious
ego, 188
Insight, and assimilation of